# HOW TO HELP YOUR SPOUSE HEAL FROM YOUR AFFAIR

## A Guide to Regaining Trust, Resolving Conflict and Rebuilding Your Marriage

### LORAINE HUMPHREY

# TABLE OF CONTENTS

# INTRODUCTION

"My spouse does not understand that my pain is real and my wounds are deep." ... "We should put everything behind us and start our relationship again."

These are recurrent statements from a partner who has cheated.

After confessing the betrayal, they readily stated that they felt an immediate sense of relief. The people involved have probably kept the secret about the extramarital affair over a long period of time, ranging from weeks to months, or perhaps even years. People may feel a sense of release from their feelings of shame or guilt. There is no longer a need to remain hidden. In contrast, the spouse who has been betrayed experiences apprehension that the most feared scenario has actually materialized. The paradigm shifts dramatically. Navigating this situation can be extremely challenging and emotionally taxing, as individuals lack the knowledge and skills to effectively maneuver within it. The irrationality of the circumstances can generate deep emotional distress for one individual, while the other partner simultaneously feels a sense of comfort. The unfaithful partner must recognize that the act of confessing or being found out does not absolve him or her of the responsibility to maintain loyalty and honesty to the spouse. Ideally, it is essential to cultivate a sense of presence and caring toward the partner. In the pages of this book, all the insights and knowledge related to this topic are laid out. The author invites both parties involved in the relationship to embark on a journey of healing and recovery. It is essential to cultivate an understanding of the negative consequences experienced by individuals upon the revelation of betrayal. The potential effects on mental health can be significant. Individuals who are enduring significant distress may reach a point where they are in a state of psychological collapse. Both spouses may suffer when faced with the challenge of managing distress. In cases of intense distress, they may resort to various "coping" mechanisms, such as engaging in activities to occupy time, consuming alcohol or exhibiting disruptive behavior in the presence of their close relatives. These actions are often taken in an attempt to mask shame and guilt. Another plausible outcome is the development of feelings of bitterness and resentment toward the partner who has been unfaithful. This situation can lead to immobilization of the couple. Individuals who have been betrayed may experience feelings of frustration because of the perception that they do not have access to complete information. While those who have engaged in unfaithful behavior may show an unwillingness to cooperate. Each will experience some degree of bitterness in this particular circumstance. The absence of self-awareness may lead to personal frustration. It is likely that both individuals will not consistently exhibit behaviors conducive to healing. However, there is a distinction between remaining trapped and simply going down the path of resentment. The final decision to stay or run is uniquely up to you. A significant number of people choose to persist in a state of bitterness, shirking personal responsibility for their own emotional well-being. Especially when you become the target of another person's obvious lack of moral principles. Therefore, it is imperative to overcome this particular phase, as a more favorable outcome lies ahead. Following the experience of enduring significant pain, individuals are likely to develop a greater capacity to experience and express love in a deeper way. Affection and attachment will occur while encountering various obstacles or situations. In due course, individuals will reach a significant optimal state characterized by interpersonal bonds and general satisfaction. The influence of a person's upbringing and family background on his or her existence is of considerable importance. Most problematic individuals come from family backgrounds characterized by conflict and guilt. Lack of communication may have hindered and affected personal discussions and romantic relationships. The person's conditioning seems to inhibit the open expression of personal emotions, resulting in potential discomfort in the face of others' emotional expressions. Reflect on whether you have had the opportunity to express your personal desires and expectations or whether your focus has been primarily on fulfilling the desires and expectations of others. Evaluate whether your upbringing prioritized loyalty to others or emphasized self-interest. Commonly it is recommended that you pursue your own desires and engage in activities that provide personal satisfaction. This statement is made without considering the potential repercussions on the people you care about. You are a member of a large community, so you cannot always pursue your own interests without considering those of others. Did the people who protected you teach you to love? Were you allowed to cry or laugh within your family? Were you groped, squeezed, beaten, or otherwise violated? What was the nature of relationship conflicts in the family? What was your position within the family? What did you look for when you left your family? Whether it is the need for space or the desire to escape, or the desire for safety, security, and love, these questions are fundamental to the formation of your relationships. How you react to deception depends on the complexity of your past. In relationships, we all need both stability and adventure. But one of the two may be more important than the other. Attachment can be rooted in security, insecurity or anxiety. The ability to rely on someone who can share your anxiety and happiness can help. Secure attachment is when we have a person who gives us enough space to explore and is always there for us. With this foundation, a relationship will not break down regardless of circumstances. In the absence of this, an individual may develop an insecure attachment. An example is constant checking on the other person, chasing, conflicts to get his or her attention, etc. One can become the pursuer in the relationship, that is, the one who always wants more and often needs to be reassured of the partner's intentions. Or one can be a wait-and-see, a person who constantly rejects conflict and discussion. The behavior you enact in relationships is the result of experiences you have had in the past. You may have learned to purposely avoid getting too close to avoid disappointment. This becomes a problem when you implement it with a person who genuinely cares about us and loves us deeply. We relate to this person thinking back to the past, when we thought it was safer to keep a safe distance to protect ourselves. Generally, the strategies devised at the time to cope with a particular situation were useful at the time, but now they may be obsolete.

# 01
## RELATIONSHIPS AND INFIDELITY

**A** fulfilling career, healthy relationships, and a high standard of living are just a few of the many elements that make up a successful life. We may give more importance to one over another in our lives, but we cannot completely ignore any of them. Each of these elements completes a person's world. One can face a busy day at work with a smile if one has a strong, happy and loyal relationship. When a person is in love, everything seems easier. You and your partner discuss problems so that they do not seem like a big deal. Every person needs a healthy relationship in his or her life. Every species on the planet wants to safeguard itself. The frontal lobe of the brain helps us think clearly, ensure our safety and regulate impulses. Human attachment is another element that makes us feel safe. Children attach to parents to feel protected, and to communicate their feelings and ideas. As children we need parents or other people to take care of us. Adults also need a person to become attached to. Some people keep their distance from feelings and cannot understand relationships. They prefer to be alone and avoid commitment. It is a matter of preference. Most people think they will find a partner who will be the key to their happiness. One can meet the ideal partner in high school, at work, on the train or randomly. Today, in a technologically advanced world with little free time, many people put their pride aside and get online dating. Just logging on to a few sites is enough to find a date, although sometimes the failure can be immediate and tangible. Online dating offers a variety of options and opportunities.

Science says we are constantly looking for potential alternatives to our current mate. Researchers began examining this question about 50 years ago in an attempt to determine what motivates people to stay in a couple, or to seek alternatives. This sheds light on a number of issues. John Thibaut and Harold Kelley's theory of interdependence was a popular theory in the past. They argued that underlying emotional dependence are two processes. The first is fulfillment. This measures how well the partner satisfies your primary needs. The second factor is the standard of alternatives, which indicates how attractive a new relationship is compared to the one you are in. The investment scale is a related notion that can help you understand relationships. According to this view, emotional resources and investments made during the course of a relationship will be lost if it ends. The loss is proportional to the investment you made at the beginning. The fact that both theories are based on an alternative option is a crucial finding in this context. Being able to find an ideal partner is something that mostly everyone values and desires. When we find ourselves in a deep and fulfilling bond, we tend to underestimate this aspect. However, we start looking for the ideal substitute as soon as the security starts to fail. There has been a significant change in the dating and relationship landscape, and divorce is no longer seen as shameful. Rejecting failed relationships is more common than accepting successful ones, and the biggest drama, however, is adultery. A couple affected by adultery finds themselves in a completely new and sometimes devastating situation of suffering. It is one of the worst feelings a couple has to face. The most common reason for relationship breakdown is infidelity, which has become much more common in recent years. The person you have spent several years with, your partner or spouse who has been your rock, has had an extramarital affair, and cheated on you. This is a horrible situation to deal with! Anger is the first feeling in these circumstances. After that comes contempt and disgust. A betrayal of trust in your partnership has occurred. In a relationship, two people share feelings and emotions that are the basis for having a happy and fulfilling relationship. Then after perhaps years of living together and sharing, you choose to leave everything behind to find comfort and share your life with another person. A deleterious emotional and psychological shock can set in for the betrayed person. It hits as hard as a punch in the face. The betrayer may claim that it was only an isolated incident, but that is an excuse that has little basis; the betrayal has now been there. Emotional infidelity is something else, and for a long time it was not considered cheating, but perhaps it is even worse than physical.

Sexual intimacy is not essential in this situation, although it may be present. Another person becomes important, and it is no longer the partner, to share life and thoughts with. It can become a strong bond, and the emotions involved are very deep and intimate. Usually the person who cheats does not initially have sexual relations with the person with whom they have a romantic relationship, but they are on the verge of doing so. However, many feelings and emotions are present. It would be easy for the betrayer to claim that it is only a bond of intimate friendship and confuse the victim by labeling his or her claims as illogical. The betrayed party does not yet know if there has been a real betrayal of trust and feelings. When the betrayer refuses to acknowledge his/her mistake and the deceived party suffers inwardly and cannot express his/her doubts, the relationship deteriorates and ends. It would not be incorrect to say that, compared to a sexual relationship, this form of intimacy is much more difficult to salvage. One trait of betrayal is individualism, and it can vary depending on the circumstances. For one person, what they would consider infidelity may not be infidelity for another. Everything that happens in our lives is influenced by the reactions and responses of those close to us. It is a statistic that more than 40% of people have thoughts of suicide after a failed relationship. Those who have been betrayed have a very difficult time trusting others, including their partner, because the bond becomes a labyrinth. The emotion plunges one into depressive episodes, and one may no longer trust others. The individual also experiences self-doubt and becomes less confident in assessing the character of others. The combination of grief and anger is a persistent feeling that is difficult to overcome.

# 02

## TODAY'S SOCIETY IS PERFECT FOR TRAITORS

Even compared to the last decade alone, the world has completely changed. Communication has become very easy thanks to social media platforms and apps such as Tinder, Bumble and others. When communication is easy, emotional connections can be made in no time. These connections turn into relationships, but because they are less tangible, they may not last long. This is what experts usually note, although it is not a definitive statement. Again, it is not solely the fault of the online dating environment. Personal preferences have a profound effect. Only about 17 percent of online relationships end in marriage. Rules have always been present in relationships or marriages. It must be mutually understood and clear what is considered friendship and what crosses the line. In the last decade, these rules have changed significantly.

In 2023, there have been about 360 million Facebook users, 69 million Twitter users, more than a billion Instagram users, and so on. It is possible to access a person's photos and a significant part of his or her life simply by Googling his or her name. With this knowledge, it is relatively easier to start a conversation, process it carefully, leave an impression and develop a relationship. A person might think about looking for another partner online if they have met their current partner on some social platform or site. Even if you start a conversation with a stranger without the intention of cheating on your partner, the conversation may go beyond friendship without your knowledge. Perhaps in your head you have already imagined that you may have a relationship with this person in the future. It is possible to become immediately intimate after falling in love with someone's words.

There is a segment of society that practices gender domination and considers it acceptable to cheat on one's spouse while still legally married. It is unfortunate that some people think it is acceptable to have relationships with more than one person, hiding behind the cloak of culture and religion. The problem is not just the fact that one sex is allowed to have multiple partners, but rather the forbidden dance of the opposite. There is no doubt that cultural dominance and precedent in families of origin contribute to this narcissism. In different parts of the world, adultery is considered morally acceptable. The success or failure of our relationships determines the caliber of our lives. The love we receive from our parents, our friends and, finally, our partner, has a major influence on our lives.

The relationship of a couple has undergone a significant change in recent times. It used to be based on reproduction and sexuality, now on desire, lust and bonding. Couples support each other financially, socially and in other areas, such as raising children and maintaining a comfortable standard of living. Today's couples face more pressures than ever before, but starting a relationship requires fewer prerequisites. Because of the complexity of the circumstances involved, it is difficult to analyze a couple and break down each problem because they have gone through so many different experiences. There is no school of relationships. Because of the lack of a support system from others, many people experience doubts at various times in the relationship and have no one to turn to for guidance. Imagine the pressure of someone who falls in love in their twenties and hopes the relationship will last for the next fifty years with passion, commitment and unconditional love. Face-to-face communication is sorely lacking when it comes to developing meaningful relationships.

Since the invention of television, cell phones, laptops and countless other devices, we spend less time communicating with our partners, and more time using technology. The most important issues in life are discussed via text message and then we complain about miscommunication. When people desire the relationship of their dreams, they should also instill the tenacity needed to make it work. For a couple to endure the difficulties involved in a relationship, they must learn to grow through struggles, including ups and downs, arguments and betrayals. And it is precisely this spirit that is lacking. Most people have difficulty identifying a relationship as perfect, ideal. If you want to build a successful business, you have to fall in love with your customers, see the world through their eyes and consistently deliver quality. Likewise, these are parameters to follow for those who want to enter into a fulfilling intimate relationship. So let us begin by talking about relationship problems. Problems begin to emerge when the focus in a relationship shifts from what is given to what is received. Couples go to therapy to improve their relationships; not simply to look deeper into their lives. People are not generally inclined to change who they are. What needs to change is the belief that "you are responsible for my happiness and because of you I am unhappy." You and your partner are drifting apart because of your anger and resentment at this idea. The estrangement could then lead to infidelity because another person will come in and understand you better than your partner.

In this virtual age, there are many options available compared to decades ago when the only option was to meet face-to-face. It is incredibly easy to create a password for your phone and change it periodically, connect with new people online, and delete phone conversations. Because cheating is now easy, some people try to take advantage of the situation rather than focus on the issues present in the relationship and seek a solution. On the Internet, it is easy for people to lie and get away with it. It is very common for people to invent false personal information about age, preferences, height, weight, or any other aspect of their lives. Today's society has a great influence on the way people think and act. It is possible that people have always had the cheating "gene" but, due to lack of opportunity, have not had the courage to put it into practice. In the end, society and the betrayer are both responsible and guilty. It is unfair to hold one person truly and solely responsible.

# 03
## THERE IS NO GENDER OR AGE FOR BETRAYAL

Each individual has distinct characteristics and qualities that differentiate him or her from others. During the transition from youth to adulthood, individuals are exposed to a series of social precepts that become ingrained in their consciousness. An individual's life is influenced by a range of cultural conventions, religious beliefs and personal inclinations. The prevalence of failed marriages, divorces and dysfunctional relationships is a widespread problem in contemporary society. Everyone's life path presents different obstacles that must be faced and overcome. During adolescence, individuals confront personal fears and external influences as they navigate the process of self-discovery and sexual orientation alignment. At this developmental stage, relationships have the potential to be more exploratory and innovative due to the increased sensitivity associated with this age. Potential future relationships could be influenced and shaped by unstable bonds or adverse encounters. Jealousy and immaturity are inherent aspects of human nature that cannot be evaded. This period represents a time of seeking independence and exploring new experiences. Experiencing the state of youth and autonomy evokes a deep sense of inner exhilaration. Parents' effort to control their children's conduct is perceived as a form of submission. Adolescents often show a reluctance to listen to parental advice and abide by rules. The inclination toward a carefree, autonomous, unrestrained state of mind can cloud their judgment, potentially leading young people to pursue similar behaviors in subsequent interpersonal relationships. The prospect of engaging with a single individual may appear less appealing in the face of a seemingly boundless range of alternatives. Individuals seek autonomy and independence within their interpersonal ties, so the presence of constraints can lead to the deterioration of these relationships and friendships. Young people who are in the early stages of a romantic relationship and wish to start a family encounter a spectrum of emotional responses. Developing a relationship requires overcoming several barriers. Factors that contribute to the success of a relationship include establishing positive relationships with their respective families, managing financial matters effectively, and demonstrating acceptance of one's partner. An individual may find themselves compelled to seek a path to liberation because of their inherent desire to be relieved of these ongoing responsibilities and duties. Each person has a personal definition of the concept of freedom. Plus, there is a subset of individuals who possess the capacity to resist temptation, while another subset lacks this capacity.

Some may often find themselves attracted to those who provide comfort and respite from monotony when challenges or a flat existence arise. Those who choose to abstain from marriage may have fears about taking on important responsibilities. Because of their reluctance to commit to serious, long-term unions, these individuals show a greater propensity to engage in several relationships in their lives. During the middle years of a person's life, it is common for adults who have been engaged in a long-term relationship to have a fixed pattern or routine. According to its definition, a routine refers to a prescribed sequence of actions that are performed on a recurring basis. The phenomenon of becoming trapped in a monotonous routine is widely frowned upon, yet a significant proportion of individuals find themselves in this situation. This particular scenario represents one of the most unfavorable outcomes in a romantic relationship. When an individual experiences the loss of something while possessing all the necessary resources, the phenomenon becomes difficult to understand, leading to doubts about the relationship and a desire to explore alternative options. As a result, individuals strive to find in another individual the charm and fervor that seems to have diminished in their previous romantic involvement. To seek a sense of novelty that is absent in relationships with women of equal or older age, men direct their attention to younger women. It is like reliving one's adolescence. In contrast, a woman who is approaching menopause and experiencing uncertainty about her own femininity and attractiveness seeks to establish a connection with another individual to rekindle libido and recover a sense of desirability. The individual shows a strong desire for recognition, thus indicating a willingness to capitalize on all available opportunities that may arise.

It is widely believed that men have a greater propensity for infidelity than women. However, in contemporary society, women have similar behaviors to their male counterparts, thus establishing a sense of equality in this particular area. Men many times are unfaithful because they become trapped in a monotonous or unrewarding routine. They may feel undervalued or dissatisfied. There is also the possibility that they acquire an addiction to pornography. In the context of interpersonal relationships, it could be argued that there is a lack of personal space or autonomy. Women who experience feelings of insecurity, particularly in relation to the aging process or bodily transformations, may practice infidelity. Compared to their male counterparts, women generally exhibit higher levels of accommodation and are more susceptible to greater social and familial demands. It is possible for women to be faced with an excessive amount of demands, leading them to try to avoid or evade them. The individual in question may have a belief that her partner is not providing her with the adequate level of affection and attention to which she is entitled. The individual's sexual desires are not being fulfilled by her partner. It is possible that she may experience feelings of boredom from time to time. Based on statistical data, it is observed that most individuals, specifically 53%, who commit infidelity are in a marital relationship. Only 6% of those who commit infidelity acknowledge their involvement in an extramarital relationship. When men learn of their partner's infidelity, they tend to break off the relationship at a rate 22% higher than in cases where the roles are reversed. About 35% of women show a reluctance to take proactive measures because of a state of denial of their partners' extramarital involvements. It has been suggested that women possess a greater aptitude for deception than men, which allows them to engage in infidelity more effectively. Women's propensity for dishonesty is the same as men's. Significant communication breakdown occurs within a romantic relationship if both individuals have committed infidelity. Effective communication is a key component of any interpersonal bond, and it helps prevent future problems of adultery. Disagreements arise when communication in a relationship is sterile, and concerns and problems are hidden in an attempt to protect the other party involved. This phenomenon leads to the accumulation of emotions, which eventually culminates in intense conflict, giving rise to significant disputes.

Dealing with numerous difficulties simultaneously is less effective than solving problems sequentially, one at a time. Through the resolution of each disagreement, disparity remains constant, but understanding and compatibility gradually evolve. However, keeping uncertainties in one's thoughts and tolerating questionable or unsatisfactory behavior from the other partner only depletes the individual's emotional investment in the bond. It is possible that the partner may not be able to meet financial needs. Most individuals have a conspicuously materialistic orientation, openly expressing a desire to satisfy their personal needs. Individuals aspire to achieve a specific level of material well-being and derive satisfaction from engaging in consumer transactions. Contrary to prevailing stereotypes, it is important to recognize that men can also exhibit gold-digging behavior, similar to that of women. The prevalence of men relying on others is comparable to that of women. Individuals' stress levels may be influenced by various factors, including financial obligations such as loans, child care expenses or education costs. In addition, the presence of a demanding spouse can further exacerbate stress levels, creating an additional burden to manage. Before starting a relationship, it is essential to engage in a thorough discussion of financial issues to ensure that both people involved have their own footing. Both parties involved must be able to meet the needs of the other. People may feel pressured to abandon their current situation and pursue alternative opportunities because of persistent conflicts and miscommunication. Given the abundance of opportunities available, it is widely recognized that the state of unhappiness is very often challenged. The need for personal growth is primary in individuals. In the event that a couple fails to address problems, it is likely that one or both partners may seek comfort and companionship outside the relationship, with someone who aligns more closely with their perspectives. However, it is plausible to predict that individuals may develop emotions for another more suitable person if recurrent conflicts persist and remain unresolved.

The experience of abuse, whether manifested as physical or mental harm, results in the erosion of a person's capacity for affection and emotional attachment. Individuals who experience abusive relationships experience significant levels of suffering. Emotional abuse is characterized by manipulation, control, and isolation. The partner significantly impedes the partner's growth, and creates high levels of tension and anxiety. There are various elements that can contribute to the development of such behavior, such as a negative reputation in the workplace, diminished self-esteem, pervasive animosity, and other influences. In such cases, it is imperative that the other party promptly initiates an exit plan. The experience of physical abuse generally elicits an immediate response of aversion toward others. Breaking off such a relationship is an inevitable outcome, although leaving an emotionally abusive relationship may present difficulties. A person who seems to have kind intentions or who has a long-standing relationship with the individual in question may offer comfort and a sense of familiarity.

The likelihood of engaging in cheating appears to increase in direct correlation with the duration of the misconduct. Overcoming cheating can be a daunting task because of the considerable emotional and psychological upheaval involved. People who experience cheating deep down develop feelings of serious self-doubt. The worry arising from the perception of inadequacy is a lasting and distressing phenomenon. Later, in response to the perceived injustice of the situation, a considerable degree of anger may be unleashed. The human brain is influenced by apprehension about an ambiguous and precarious future. In some circumstances it is natural to contemplate starting a new chapter in one's life. It may pose a greater challenge than remaining anchored in the past. Codependency is an observed phenomenon prevalent in lasting relationships, and it presents significant difficulties in the resolution process. The individual experiences a state of perplexity, irritation and disturbance due to the presence of opposing feelings arising from the inability to coexist with the strong aversion to him or her. The way individuals react to acts of betrayal varies at different stages of life. During the adolescent years, the victim tends to exhibit the highest levels of violence and recklessness. Those who are affected may have a higher risk of developing suicidal or major depressive tendencies due to their limited level of emotional and psychological development. When a young person encounters an act of betrayal, a process of self-doubt begins. The basis of each subsequent relationship is influenced by the experience of a previous failed relationship. During adulthood, upon the occurrence of an act of infidelity, people often show a tendency to suppress or minimize the event. Both parties engage in mature discourse in an attempt to ascertain whether it is more prudent to maintain their marital union or pursue a legal dissolution of marriage. In most cases, the couple has offspring, who are placed first by each parent. The children assume a prominent position, receive significant attention, and their welfare becomes the main and essential object.

# 04
## PREMONITORY SIGNS OF BETRAYAL

O ne must trust one's intuitions and feelings. The prevalence of adultery cases sometimes remains hidden due to failure to detect the betrayal. Affective blindness may bring the inability to perceive the act of infidelity. However, it is necessary to observe certain peculiarities in the behavior of those who commit adultery. Failure to recognize the indicators and remaining in a state of denial can lead to greater damage to one's psyche than dealing with the problem. The accumulation of falsehoods and unethical actions reaches a threshold that becomes increasingly difficult to ignore, resulting in decreasing the likelihood of the relationship remaining in place. It is essential to observe these subtle clues without arousing suspicion. There are numerous methods for determining whether a partner is unfaithful;

however, it is essential to have a complete understanding of the situation. Certain atypical behaviors exhibited by a spouse should not automatically be interpreted as indicative of infidelity or emotional involvement with another individual. It is essential to take a global perspective and analyze alterations in behavioral patterns. It is important to be patient to understand the motivations behind an event that deviates from normalcy. The partner may show a sudden inclination toward possessiveness toward the cell phone, laptop, or any other electronic device. Another abnormal behavior may be refusing access to such devices. One should be alarmed when the level of secrecy increases from before, and this may clearly signify their reluctance to ascertain the identity of the people with whom they communicate. In an age of extensive technological advances, keeping secrets and close relationships with others has become increasingly easy. Cell phones have emerged as crucial tools to foster and sustain connections and relationships. Another wake-up call may be changing "historical" passwords, or not using the devices in your presence. It is important to exercise caution if you are in the presence of late-night phone calls and a consequent increase in secrecy about the caller's identity. It is not advisable, however, to develop an obsessive inclination to monitor your spouse's mobile device, with the intent of detecting any clues to potential extramarital involvement.

There often seems to be a noticeable change in a spouse's sartorial choices or increased concern for his or her physical appearance when adultery is present. It is possible that she devotes more time to exercise with the intention of improving his or her physical fitness. In addition, individuals may deliberately choose aesthetically pleasing and elegant clothing for seemingly informal social occasions. This is not necessarily indicative of a person seeking social interaction, but if these circumstances occur within the daily routine, they may serve as potential indicators. Should such circumstances occur, it is recommended to maintain vigilance and closely monitor the spouse's actions, while attempting to engage in an open dialogue about any concerns. Enthusiasm for social outings or jointly watching a favorite Netflix series, which previously constituted a shared activity, seems to diminish. The tendency to deviate from previously jointly agreed plans increases. The partner committing infidelity provides justifications to avoid meeting you or consistently ignores your phone calls without you having committed any actual wrongdoing. In this scenario, it is advisable to give the benefit of the doubt to those involved, but to judge any unusual occurrences rationally. However, if the behavior persists and seems to indicate a lack of interest or rejection, it is plausible to consider the presence of a third person within the relationship.

Changes in a partner's usual routine and preferences are another sign of potential infidelity. One noticeable change in your partner's behavior involves the engagement ring. Has he/she stopped wearing it altogether or does he/she remove it more often? This indication is considered passive and does not require much attention or concern. However, if it occurs in conjunction with other abnormal changes, it may warrant a more vigilant and critical approach. If people in one's social circle perceive alterations in the dynamics of a relationship and express apprehension about the way those involved interact, this may be an indication of potential problems within that bond. Considerable alteration in behavior or habits may occur, such as adopting new speech patterns or using previously unaccustomed vocabulary. The partner may begin to engage in an alternative genre of music from those loved ones, or change tastes in other areas as well. Unlike previously, they change habits with schedules. The factors mentioned above are not tangible evidence that one's partner has a preference for another individual. However, a person who sticks to a strict routine may raise concerns if there is a sudden alteration in his or her conduct or habitual practices. It may happen that the individual shows a sudden inclination toward a new pastime or hobby that did not previously arouse his or her interest. It is possible to observe changes toward positions in the political or other sphere, even on those they previously firmly supported. The presence of unaccounted-for expenses in the partner's financial records, or the potential suggestion of establishing customized banking arrangements, may give rise to investigation. There are several variations of this phenomenon. It is advisable to remain vigilant regarding atypical banking transactions. One should closely monitor the frequency of their ATM withdrawals and be vigilant in cases where suspicions arise or their behavior appears mysterious. A search should be made for any hotel reservations or regular deposits made to an unknown account. It is imperative not to overlook the presence of new and expensive assets, especially when unable to provide a full account of their origin or acquisition. Unclear money transactions are indicative of clandestine activities within a relationship and are one of the most common behaviors. To deal effectively with such circumstances, it is advisable to give the person suspected of infidelity the opportunity to give the benefit of the doubt or conceal the truth, so as to allow for a discreet investigation without alarming the other party involved. Other suspicious behavior is the habit of taking unexplained trips for business or with friends, showing reluctance to disclose specific travel information. People may begin to extend work hours into the evening and even devote time on weekends to work-related activities. Arguments within the relationship may increase, and the one who cheats has a habit of placing all the blame for the lost harmony on the betrayed, excluding himself or herself from any responsibility.

Another significant indicator of cheating is the lack of sexual interest towards the original partner. Try to ascertain the causes of the decline in sexual activity within the relationship, but remain alert to any discernible alteration in behavior. This phenomenon may be an indication or a causal factor contributing to the deterioration of the relationship. In cases where a couple cannot openly communicate their sexual demands or if either partner fails to meet them, it is plausible that there may be a decline in the emotional bond, leading to a search for a more compatible partner. Both men and women show assertiveness in seeking desired qualities in a potential partner. Sexual decline is a common occurrence in the context of marital relationships. Once a couple becomes parents or becomes involved in the complexities of life, maintaining the same degree of sexual desire can be difficult. A couple is more likely to separate, however, when feelings of love diminish or cease to exist, rather than because of a lack of sexual activity. In such cases, one of the two individuals may be inclined to seek companionship in another person who is willing to fill the emotional gaps missing in the current relationship. It would not be inaccurate to say that those who maintain a closed attitude toward their sexuality are prone to experience an escalation of inequality, ultimately increasing the likelihood of relationship dissolution. There is a difference in the way people relate today compared to the past. People may not make eye contact during conversations and may refrain from implementing habitual behaviors such as kissing before going to work or other similar routines. Changes in habits are to be rationally monitored and analyzed. Partners may begin to show a tendency to disregard their obligations, creating an emotional and physical distance between them and their children or other members of the family network. Parents may decide to refuse the responsibility of picking their children up from school or accompanying them to classes, refrain from attending school meetings, or refuse to spend more time with them. To cultivate a successful and mutually beneficial interpersonal relationship, it is essential to establish a foundation of trust in which one feels comfortable and secure, to allow the partner to access one's own emotional vulnerability. Undoubtedly one must possess a comprehensive knowledge of one's partner. One can observe distinct behavioral responses exhibited by the individual in question when experiencing emotions such as happiness, anger, tension, fatigue or boredom. However, as mentioned earlier, the most obvious behavior that indicates infidelity in an individual is the manifestation of an attitude that deviates from the usual one. The individual's habitual conduct, daily regimen, and behaviors undergo a transformation.

An indicator of infidelity in a male partner in particular is diverting their complete attention and focus from the relationship. The level of interest and investment in the well-being and shared experiences as a couple tends to decline. If a partner shows sudden emotional detachment, it is plausible to consider the potential occurrence of infidelity in the relationship. We can argue that if an individual has engaged in cheating behaviors in the past, he or she is likely to continue to do so in the future. There are two distinct categories of individuals who engage in cheating behaviors. The first category includes those individuals who feel deep remorse and guilt for their actions. The second category includes those characterized by narcissistic tendencies who display cheating behaviors without having any remorse. The individual shows a propensity to enact deceptive behaviors and is able to maintain a second relationship without problems. Research has indicated that if the quality and duration of your intimate and rewarding experiences as a couple have decreased significantly, appearing hurried, distracted and lacking interest, it is possible that your partner is having an extramarital affair.

Partners who engage in deceptive behavior often show a tendency to provide an excessive amount of perhaps unsolicited information during discussions with their partner. Another indicator of untrue statements is body language. Repeatedly touching the nose, covering the mouth, fidgeting or shaking anxiously may indicate a tendency to withhold information or hide something. Another possible significant sign of infidelity is the habit of mispronouncing a partner's name. It is not uncommon for the identity of the individual with whom one is committing infidelity to emerge inadvertently in conversations, sometimes even in circumstances deemed inappropriate. The sudden emergence of an increased need for personal privacy can be considered abnormal and alarming. Monitoring his or her company is advisable, this is because close social ties, including friends and colleagues, exert an influence on behavior. Generally, those who engage in cheating behavior tend to associate with other individuals who in turn engage in such behavior. Women seek in their partners a confidant, a person with whom they can share their problems and emotions. When this is missing, they tend to seek emotional comfort elsewhere, with a friend or colleague. So if a woman no longer shows any interest in your day-to-day life or turns out to be less involved, it is possible that she is looking for a deeper, more involved connection. This is because women are naturally caring, so if she behaves with less sensitivity toward you, she is most likely no longer as interested in you. If, knowing her usual movements, she plans to meet people you have never heard of or is unable to explain with whom she has spent time, she is likely cheating on you. A change in work schedule or a tendency to stay away from home more should make you suspicious. Also, if he obsessively asks what time you will be home, or what your daily schedule is, this may be a sign of a possible extramarital affair.

# 05

## HOW TO COPE WITH BETRAYAL

The experience of betrayal is considered a deeply distressing event for anyone. The potential outcomes can have severe and far-reaching impacts. At the initial moment, a multitude of emotions emerge, and there is a mix of emotionality and frustration. The question, "why did this happen," pervades the minds of those who have been betrayed. Typically, suspicions precede the event. Even if a person is aware and prepared to deal with the fact, the trauma is still very strong. When the person you have invested in admits that they have deceived you, the realization hits like a hurricane. You experience a mixture of highly explosive emotions that leave a deep wound in the psyche. You try not to let post-traumatic stress overwhelm you. You lose sleep, struggle to concentrate, lose weight, and may go to extremes such as depression or suicidal thoughts. In a perfect world, no one would want to experience the heartbreak that follows infidelity. However, the truth is hard to face. Some individuals fall into depression, cry for hours, and reflect on the reasons that led to this situation. The initial reaction may also be to run away from the shock and shut down. A decision is made not to acknowledge the infidelity, labeling it as a misunderstanding or simple overreaction. Both the infidel and the betrayed experience pain, confusion, and a flood of emotions that must be dealt with. The pain intensifies in proportion to the couple's involvement. In the psyche of the betrayed person, denial, anger, and moments of acceptance alternate. The term "bargaining" refers to vacillating thoughts about "what if." Different thoughts are interspersed in the mind. "Maybe it will come back if I lose weight and become more attractive"... "everything will work out if we go to a counselor" ... etc.

Like the betrayed, the unfaithful person can also experience loss. As soon as he/she observes his/her partner's behavior, they may conclude that the relationship is irretrievably broken. The betrayed person begins to doubt everything and crave security. They may become hostile in response to the sense of abandonment. They may fixate on small details and experience increased isolation and distress. If the unfaithful person is going to recover the relationship, regain lost trust, and gain forgiveness from the partner, they will face a complicated and laborious period. The partner will ask every little detail about everything, vent, feel anguish and distress. They must try to make the betrayed person feel safe in those moments of initial panic. It is essential to keep in mind that the individual is experiencing an intimate violation at this time. Real or perceived makes no difference. It is a biological reaction that cannot be rationalized, at least in the initial moment. A key aspect is to think about how to help them. Absolutely avoid becoming combative, but admit one's own shortcomings and faults. This is very difficult to accomplish, since the interlocutor may be fighting, and the natural response to conflict is defense. A process of dialogue is needed between the afflicted partner and the unfaithful partner to better understand their emotions. The priority should be to improve their level of emotional and psychological well-being. One must be present, sit with them and help them overcome their distress. After dealing with the circumstance, another possible response is avoidance. This could be a physical or emotional retreat, where the person withdraws completely. The immediate thought of harming and betraying the unfaithful person may come to mind. The impulse to return the ill-gotten gains to the unfaithful spouse is a normal reaction.

Unfaithful people may hastily conclude that their relationship is over. They may interpret this as the last indication that their partner will leave and easily move on to something else, while it may simply be a coping mechanism for the trauma caused. It is a safety-seeking behavior that only serves to cope with the traumatic circumstances. The pendulum of emotions whereby one day you want to get intimate and the next day you want to break off the relationship are all reactions caused by the adrenaline rush received. After discovering your partner's infidelity, being confused is completely normal. However, you must come out of apathy and experience these emotions. Do not repress your feelings. You will not benefit from letting your emotions build up. Record your experiences in a journal or on paper. Give yourself a break, and avoid anything that reminds you of the individual. If you are currently cohabitating, you should separate for a while. If you are in a long-term relationship, avoid talking to the unfaithful person. Social media may be something to avoid, and try to avoid stalking or looking at photos of you together. Try to divert your attention elsewhere. Undertaking different activities or joining a gym to get in shape are common practices.

As an initial response, do not denigrate your partner, create scenes in the family, or file for divorce immediately. This impulse may later lead to remorse, but it should not be interpreted as a suggestion of acceptance or absolution. There is no absolute form of punishment, and revenge can only temporarily cure the "thirst" for revenge. It does more harm than good. There is no greater satisfaction than that which comes from being on the side of reason, and the advice is to wait for the situation to stabilize by forcing the perpetrator to repent on his/her own. To manage the agony, seek comfort from someone, because it is impossible to overcome the anguish and discomfort caused by an act of infidelity in a single day. You can rely on a friend or your parents, or, if you do not feel comfortable talking about your problems, you can consult a psychiatrist. Begin the rehabilitation process by expressing your true feelings. Consider your emotional improvement as your primary goal. Try to avoid negative thoughts, and above all, stay away from anything that can remind you of them. It is difficult but essential to put it into action. Cry, take action, go out with friends, stay late, celebrate, plan a vacation or buy something you wanted but always put off. The whole purpose is to ensure the healing of your soul and spirit with minimal risk to your health. Try to avoid contact with their close relatives or people close to them. Take enough time before you resume contact with the person. Face it with courage. Be firm when you meet him or her and do not return in a state of confusion and apprehension. Examine the mistakes you have made. When you have had time to recover, investigate the causes that brought you into this situation. Consider your long-term plans. Think about your children, if you have any. Don't look for another person right away. It is permissible to be angry and to make people feel the pain you have suffered. However, once you have overcome this obstacle, you should continue to move forward in your life. You can get in touch with someone who is suffering similar pain; the confrontation can be constructive. You must look for a way to progress and grow as a result of these circumstances.

If you find it difficult to come to terms with the situation, rather than moving toward something devastating, try to determine what caused the deterioration of the relationship. The focus should be on retracing your steps and identifying the indicators and causes that you believe led to the betrayal. Rarely is the flow unidirectional. Blame is to be apportioned to both, obviously with different percentages. Each partner in a failed relationship has neglected to meet the other's needs. Even if the relationship appears distant at the moment, maintain hope that it can be recovered. Do not neglect your partner's current behavior during this phase of complete confusion. The most challenging aspect is confrontation with your partner. If you intend to mend the relationship, dialogue cannot be avoided. You must engage in conversations with your partner to determine whether he or she intends to salvage the relationship. Having endured, and overcome, the impact of infidelity...Where are you both at? Are you in the direction of ending the relationship? Is there something holding you back? What details about the event do you need to know? Why did your partner need another person? Where did they first meet? You may need to consult a psychologist, a trusted acquaintance, or a family member to delve into the triggers of the illicit relationship. Now assess the situation and come to a conclusion. Examine whether they are repentant, or disinterested-this is crucial. Sometimes the unfaithful partner refuses to provide details or may not want to make amends. Don't take it to heart and don't get caught in doubt if he or she does not provide all the information you ask for. Withholding information at this time is obviously the most selfish action you can take. They have torn their partner's heart, but refuse to tell him what he deserves to know. It is like leaving someone in the shadows to solve a puzzle without providing them with the necessary information. Most likely the cheating partner is too ashamed or the details are too traumatic to talk about, and may believe that you will not be able to deal with them. When the betrayed person tries to put the pieces of the incident together, he or she is trying to get a comprehensive view. To understand the triggers, and to realize if there are possibilities for reconciliation. In an uncomfortable situation, an unfaithful person does not like to talk about his or her relationship, addiction, and decisions. However, the betrayed spouse cannot recover unless he or she resolves certain issues, and unless he or she can metabolize the affair in its entirety. Their imagination may run wild and they may begin to imagine things that did not happen. They try to put together various scenarios and visualize the worst-case scenario, which aggravates their suffering. They do not know what to forgive, continuing to remain in a state of paralysis. Many times, the unfaithful person is unable to deal with the problem because he or she is not yet totally healed. Generally, people shut down when shame takes over. They may be more afraid of reliving their mistakes than the betrayed person is of hearing information about the betrayal. There may be more to the betrayal than they have admitted so far, which is probably another reason why they keep quiet. If they reveal all the missing pieces, they believe they lose any chance of recovery. To avoid this circumstance, the betrayer must assure him or her that he or she will consider all the information and refrain from drawing hasty conclusions. If he/she wants full disclosure, and any chance of recovery, he/she must agree to it, however difficult it may be.

# 06

## CONSEQUENCES OF BETRAYAL ON CHILDREN

Undoubtedly, in a relationship that falls apart, the children suffer the most. Parents are the role models in every family. Compared to children born in the 1970s or 1980s, today's children are closer to their parents throughout childhood. Even if a relationship is problematic, parents should take responsibility for their children's upbringing by putting aside their personal conflicts, as any disruption in their children's upbringing can have a negative impact on their lives. It is crucial to examine an unsuccessful relationship through the eyes of adolescents and young adults. Here is an example of the effect on offspring from a conflicted relationship. "Although my parents are divorced, all my schoolmates think I am carefree and always happy. However, when I come home and go to bed, I lie down and cry for a long time, but no one knows. I love both of my parents. My father, my two sisters and I reside in the United States, while my mother resides in another country. I only see my mother during vacations and think of her intensely every moment." His parents divorced when he was four years old; he is now thirteen. The effects of parental separation on children depend on a number of complex circumstances and situations. Some children thrive when they are removed from conflict environments, because an unhealthy environment is not good for mental and emotional balance. Especially in the developmental and growth stage in a child. An eventual divorce has several effects on the offspring. They suffer from anxiety, melancholy, poor contact with their parents, and decline in their self-esteem. These effects persist into adulthood and can have lasting consequences. Children may continue to experience psychological difficulties and have less than ideal relationships with their partners. Most of them may end up divorced or in dysfunctional relationships influenced by the divorce they experienced as children. Parental behavior shapes their mental development. If one of the parents ends up cheating, the children may consider it acceptable behavior and reproduce it in their future relationships. Because they are too young to understand, the psychological effects of parental betrayal may leave confusion in children's minds. Conversely, a young adult may develop an aversion to the unfaithful parent, causing a strong and firm relationship to collapse. No one is born with the ability to understand and forgive a cheating parent.

In addition to parents, it is peers who have a great influence on children. It is not uncommon that they may be embarrassed by the cheating parent and be laughed at in school. Although in recent years, infidelity between partners is very common. Children may be negatively affected by repressed emotions at home and discussions they experience on a daily basis. This causes anxiety, nervous tension and decreased self-esteem. If there is a toxic environment at home and a difficult environment at school or college, children may hold back their emotions, causing emotional damage. Especially nowadays, children may experience conflicts with their peers, so they need parental guidance more than ever. Children can be cruel to each other, and social media posts can sometimes push them over the edge. This is why parenting can be critical in overcoming adverse and harmful events.

As children grow older, they may develop abandonment issues, possessive behavior, and feelings of insecurity. The fact that they live with only one parent or with an adjunct partner may cause them to desire the presence of the other parent. Anyone who later develops a friendship or relationship is burdened by the fear of experiencing something similar experienced by their parents. They lose faith in love and move cautiously before opening up to someone. They find it very difficult to place their trust in others. They may refuse to give their partner the benefit of the doubt, drawing parallels with their parents' relationship. It has been shown that children are affected by their parents' relationship according to the intensity of their conflict and involvement. For example, if parents argue and the father asks the child to inform the mother that he will not be able to attend the parents' day at school, the child will be upset. When the child gets involved in the conflict, they become part of it. This puts them in turmoil and anxiety. He/she may even feel forced to choose one faction over the other. Both parents are equally essential and dear to their children, so making a choice is difficult. Children may also feel that they are responsible for their parents' incessant quarrels and go as far as self-harm. Their problems begin when they witness their parents' quarrels, continue during the divorce process, and continue beyond that. Divorce has become widespread, and unfortunately so many children are facing it, and suffering from it. They are affected differently at each stage of the process. They must receive the same affection and attention from both parents, regardless of whether they choose co-parenting or not. Otherwise they will be permanently marked by the pain of separation. Children can still develop these problems if there is persistent conflict between parents and a lack of communication and support. Parents must recognize that their children are their top priority. They must be sensitive to their needs and engage in open dialogue about their problems. They must avoid arguing with them and involving them in their own conflicts. Children must be allowed to focus on homework and studies rather than on parental misunderstandings. Co-parenting rules should be as child-friendly as possible. The other parent should not be denigrated in front of them. Despite the failed relationship between the parents, other family members should not suffer the problems of such conflict. Keep your disagreements away from the children and raise them in a healthy and peaceful environment. Be available to answer their questions and concerns. Try to get their approval at all times and explain to them adequately what is happening around them.

Share all information and closely monitor their behavior toward you. Maintain contact with the parents of their closest peers. Take care of your children's mental health; it is most important. Their bodies reveal a lot about their emotions. Observe their eating habits. If they complain of persistent stomach aches, it is possible that they are unable to digest food properly because of suppressed emotions. The apparent reaction of a child whose parents argue is an increased heart rate. He may feel dizzy and terrified. The rush of excess stress hormones is detrimental to growth and overall health. If you are emotionally distant as a father or mother, your child may carry this trait into new relationships. Parents may be disapproving, mentally ill, substance dependent, violent, unreliable, or absent. If experienced during childhood or adolescence, your child may also exhibit one or more of these characteristics. Obviously these are negative peculiarities; for positive ones the same reasoning applies. A child, in order to grow up, must first understand who his or her parents are. In other words, children are the mirror of their parents, and they assimilate, like a sponge, everything experienced during their early years of life, and beyond. Parents are their "heroes" and children see them as role models. A divorce is a traumatic event for a child, who had always probably considered the parents an inseparable couple. They do not understand how the union between their parents could be broken. To avoid trauma, it is necessary to proceed with restraint, and explain to one's children that there is a possibility that two people may break up and sever their bond. If possible, it would be preferable to have them go through a process of psychological therapies, as it could be painful. Parental bonding is crucial for every child because it lays a foundation for peaceful emotional growth. It gives the child the confidence to go out into the world and attempt tasks that would otherwise be too challenging. If he/she lacks this element, he/she may have difficulty showing empathy or expressing emotions toward another person. He or she may decrease his or her level of familiarity with all things emotional and relational.

If emotions are suppressed due to insecurity, it is necessary to find that inner voice to express everything that is deep inside him/her. Writing it down on a piece of paper is a good idea, and it will be like a letter written by a child self to an adult self. Everything painful that has happened, all the inhibited feelings or whims. Anything that has been held back and needs to be externalized. During childhood you may have missed maternal messages that you always wanted to hear from your mother. They might be like, "I love you, unconditionally," "You are great," and "Whatever happens I am close to you." It may sound strange, but if there have been parental gaps, this introspective process will be liberating. A therapy session can be incredibly therapeutic. A specialist in attachment trauma can help address these issues and turn them into something healthy. That said, the right way to promote healing is to focus on your relationship with yourself rather than with others. Concern yourself with your own well-being, try to grow and make the best of every situation that arises.

# 07

## CALM AFTER THE STORM

After a betrayal, the relationship may end, and both parties may decide to go their separate ways. One may also choose to remain friends, but the betrayal was the final chapter that closed a loving relationship for good. It is essential for both parties to face and accept the situation. Sometimes, ending the relationship is the best option, but some couples struggle to end it permanently. The consequences of the heartbreaking moments of discovering the betrayal can be many. Concerns may arise about what decision to make, deciding whether to leave or try again. You must determine whether the relationship you are trying to salvage is the right one for you. Can you find satisfaction in the relationship? Do you still feel in your heart that you can accept the person back despite the circumstances? If you cannot answer these questions, or answer them negatively, your relationship and the current situation will likely be irreparable. Regrets may also arise. Regret that you gave up fighting when the relationship could be saved, or regret that you stayed with your partner, only to realize that the relationship was at the end of the line. But how do you determine whether a relationship is worth saving? And before that, what do you desire in a happy relationship? You need to figure out the true purpose of your life. Many agree that happiness is the purpose of people's existence. For many people, a relationship is the foundation, the pillar of their happiness. If your relationship meets your needs, it brings out your best qualities. If you do not have a fulfilling relationship, but you desire one, you will not experience integral happiness. You may not be able to realize the full potential you have to give and receive. Lacking this aspect, life can seem more difficult and you will feel deprived of genuine affection and a sense of complete well-being.

When an episode of betrayal happens in a relationship, problems of emotional stress, doubt and perplexity take over. These can detract from the importance of the other person in your life. First of all, you must be honest with yourself, learning to know yourself deeply. Strive to understand what you need in life, in the relationship or in any circumstance. It is all about putting your happiness at the center. It is not about the material goods you desire, but about emotional and mental well-being. Material objects give passing pleasure. You must open yourself to the emotions you desire for your happiness. How do you want to live your daily experiences? The questions you must ask yourself to find out what you need are what feelings are essential for you. Happiness, security, serenity, passion, intimacy, adventure, love and freedom are some examples. Consider what matters most to you. Try to summarize your life goals with a clear list. In other words, what do you want your acquaintances to say about you? What do you want your existence to mean to you and your loved ones? The next step is to list three wishes that will bring you happiness and serenity. They can be activities or anything that has a positive effect on you. Do you consider your lifestyle to be optimal? How would you ideally like to live? You may desire a penthouse in the city, or a farmhouse in the country for a simple existence in harmony with nature, or traveling the world. You may choose to desire the possession of a material good or simply have a desire to take care of your loved ones. Choices are subjective, and vary from person to person. These are some examples of what might be considered an ideal lifestyle. When you have answered all these questions, you will understand what the main desires are in your life.

If you consider your relationship to be over, and there is no more room for reconciliation, you may decide to look for a new partner. It is an escape from your current situation into a new and ideal world. Create a mental image of what you believe makes your life happy and authentic. Do not set limits for yourself. The image should represent what you and your ideal partner should do together and what emotions you should exchange. This aspect can vary widely. Some people imagine taking a mystical trip to India, some start a business together, and others change their lives by moving to some mountainous area. The next stage involves a comparison of partners. You begin by comparing your current partner with your ideal partner. This will give you an idea of whether or not your current partner is ideal for you. You can imagine their lifestyle and compare it with yours to identify any similarities. Do you share the same desires and especially the same emotions? It is essential to determine whether your desires and goals are so drastically different from those of your partner. Typically, these differences result in significant relationship problems, including lack of intimacy, arguments and conflicts. Ultimately, you must accommodate your partner's needs and vice versa. If you and your partner want different things, you must have personal space and flexibility. This is for each to achieve their ultimate goals and build a solid and reliable future. There must be a willingness to compromise.

Since emotions can fluctuate over time, it is necessary to have ongoing conversations at various stages of the relationship. Love is not determined solely by chemistry, desire or initial attraction. These characteristics evolve and change over time. Passion and love cannot be equated. To love is the ability to make the other person happy, facilitated by affection and shared values. You can remember and recount your first meeting and confess the emotions you felt when you met. Recount all the events, not to describe them to someone else, but rather to assess on what basis your love was born. Then, determine whether the values that were important at the time coincided with those of your partner. Consider your own uncertainties, discomforts, and concerns. Do you still consider them relevant? It is essential to be aware of such emotions. Try to understand the main reason why you pursued a relationship with this person. Now you need to get to the current situation, evaluate your current relationship with your partner, and figure out what has not worked. What is the main cause of all your disagreements? Do genuine feelings remain but are they overshadowed by problems? To this end, you can first list the qualities of your partner that you admire. Determine what you like and what you would like to change. After making a list, evaluate what led to the breaking point. On a scale of one to ten, give a score to each cause of the problems. The next step is to determine how challenging it will be for your partner to change their behavior in the couple. Since you desperately want them to change, assess whether there is room for change or not. These methods will allow you to understand how you feel about each other and whether your relationship has a strong foundation or whether you can consider it terminated. They also serve as a reality check on compatibility, something you may have always underestimated. Finally, you must ask yourself why you are considering saving this relationship. What is the motivation? Consider the positive reasons for your relationship. You need to reflect on its positive qualities and remember happy times. Consider your partner's best qualities and evaluate whether they still make a positive impact on you.

Fear of leaving a comfort zone may be one of the negative factors that pushes you to stay in a relationship. You may have concerns that prevent you from moving forward. Guilt, loss of dignity, concern about the opinion of family or friends, as well as financial considerations. It could be because you do not want your children to grow up in a broken home, or for religious reasons that prohibit you from leaving your partner. However, the greatest fear of all is that of being truly alone and unloved. Building on these considerations, you must now have a clear understanding of your emotions. When you have a crisp and forthright opinion, you will be able to truly understand what to do. After an initial lurch, look for a clear direction. Generally, when a marriage or relationship deteriorates and ends, people may feel that they have lost the ability to love. They conclude that their lack of happiness is due to the failed marriage and their inability to make their partner happy. They lose interest in themselves and fear further relationship failures. Some believe that leaving the partner will bring happiness and serenity. In reality, relationship deterioration can sometimes hide the symptom of having no real purpose in one's life. Having medium- and long-term plans, even shared with the partner, are the real driving force of a relationship. This will lead to seeing the relationship as beneficial. When there is a lack of stimulation in one's life, it is as if one has stopped growing. Pursuing goals generates a feeling of development and planning. Generally, when love or attraction wanes, it is because the emotional drive has ceased. The purpose that drives us to enter into relationships or marriages is to share the journey of life with another person. The initial spark or unbridled passion fades over time, but firmer values, such as respect and trust, take over. This a path that can evolve into a happy and fulfilling relationship, or to a decline characterized by loss of interest and passion. Therefore, to prevent this from happening, it is essential to focus on the relationship at hand. If necessary, modify the wrong behaviors to maintain interest and a strong feeling, and avoid being in a compromised situation.

Many people have growth as their primary goal in life, while others may pursue security. When they reach a stable point in terms of growth and development in their lives, they find that it no longer satisfies them. It is undeniable that a primary human goal is to progress and improve, and this is also true in relationships. Like a child, who the more he learns about something, the more intriguing and curious he finds it. After learning and acquiring all the necessary knowledge, he moves on to learning new information. Similarly, there must be something in a relationship that rekindles passion. The lack of this continuous flame brings barrenness and desolation where once there was lush and fertile soil. If you need revitalization, you need to reconnect emotionally with the past and the present. Sexuality plays an important role in this. Sex, in a couple's relationship, cannot be seen as something to be done twice a week in the same way for the next fifty years. No matter how well one knows the other person, it is difficult to find new ways to make a relationship exciting and engage in new activities together. In a healthy relationship, both partners need to be constantly evolving. Maintaining momentum requires a great deal of effort and concentration. Many people, for example, change jobs several times before finding stability. Change is rapid and can be beneficial. When you stay in a comfort zone for a long time, things can begin to lose some of their bite. Then, however, new opportunities emerge and growth continues. When you trace a person's career in retrospect, you may notice that for some reason he or she has moved on to the next best option. This is true development, and as it is implemented in our daily lives, you should not shy away from applying it to your relationships. To follow this discourse it is necessary to increase your awareness. This also sheds light on the pressures society puts on people. One's ego and the desire for a better existence are becoming more and more central and prioritized. Even in relationships, the future is uncharted territory, and expectations for a perfect relationship are very high, because we seek perfection. We want more from relationships, so once emotional needs are met-especially continuously-we start to question things. If you are divorcing or trying to get away from someone, there is nothing more essential than knowing your purpose.

Hartville Hendricks described something called the fuser-isolator dynamic, which involves one person running and the other chasing. The isolator unconsciously pushes others away and keeps them at a distance because the isolator needs a lot of personal space. They place immense value on freedom. The melter is the individual with an insatiable need for closeness. They desire constant group activities. If they are not satisfied in time, they begin to feel abandoned. The mere concept of divorce plunges them into a state of despondency. They need physical affection and reassurance, as well as verbal closeness. Occasionally, they may exchange responsibilities. Simply identifying themselves as the melter type or isolator type offers a great parameter for comparison. Different relationships may bring out these particular characteristics. Within the relationship, fusor energy is more aligned with feminine energy, while isolator energy is more aligned with masculine energy. Although we all possess both, the two engines of the relationship are very distinct. The fundamental principle of feminine energy is compassion. Women can remain mainly dissatisfied until this energy is recognized as love. The driving and very deep-rooted force of the masculine principle is purpose. The one who plays the role of the melter is more oriented in the space of love or the heart, unlike the isolator partner, whose focus is more on career, business or whatever. The isolator one must be aligned with a specific goal. The priority is to understand the two roles within the relationship. To get in touch with yourself and achieve your personal and couple goals, you need to do several things. To accomplish this, you need to take several steps to establish a connection with yourself. If you recognize yourself in the role of melter, you are the pursuer and your partner is the one who is more independent. Their focus is not solely on you or your family; it is elsewhere. Obviously you are the weak link in the relationship, and trying to fight this codependency will give you strength. Your sense of self will become stronger, making you less dependent on the insulator. You will feel like a series of bricks that make up the load-bearing wall of the relationship. The way they treat you will not affect you as much, and you may experience a strengthening that will help you stand on your own two feet. Your partner surprised by this change may wish to get back in touch with you.

If you are making efforts to get back with the person in question, but that person continues to ignore you or treat you badly, it is possible that they are rejecting communication. Alternatively, they may be in a new emotional or physical relationship. It is very easy to become despondent and angry if you are in this situation. The whole situation seems unreasonable and compromised. It may seem that you are making all the efforts and the other party is proceeding without any consideration or sensitivity. There are some options available in these circumstances. If your spouse wants to leave and you want to stay together, you are in one of the most difficult situations. Currently, you both desire different things. Things have changed as your initial relationship has progressed. Sometimes we overlook it, but change is a constant in life. Therefore, both your partner and the circumstances of your relationship have changed. Sometimes relationship conflicts occur and we refuse to adapt to events, and resolve them. This opposition may result from an unwillingness to embrace change. Upon reflection, we may have believed that things were better than they actually were. The first step is to acknowledge that both you and your partner have changed and that this can happen. It is completely normal. You must eliminate the expectation that your partner necessarily wants to stay with you. Putting pressure on a person is the quickest way to push them out of the relationship and away from a possible return. Keep reminding yourself that stubbornness results in more pressure, and that this pressure will cause your partner to move away. But how can you achieve a positive outcome when the person refuses to go along with your demands? You must remember that the current state of your marriage is not optimal. But you still have intense feelings, and you want a new relationship because you believe there is still room for reconciliation. However, by making some changes in your behavior, you can make sure that your partner is interested in staying with you. Relieving the pressures that are driving him or her away can be constructive.

Get rid of the idea that to be satisfied you must stay in a relationship with this person at any cost. It is obvious that you want to be with him/her and have all the benefits that come from his/her presence in your life if the thought of being separated seems devastating. However, you might abandon him/her if your outlook on life is too great an unknown. You might discover someone with whom you could have a better and happy relationship. You would prefer not to, but you might if necessary. Therefore, consider the thought that it may not be essential to be tied to your partner in order to be satisfied and happy. When you gain this insight, you will be amazed at how independent you will become and what a new perspective you will have. When things begin to change internally, they also begin to change externally. You desire to stay together and for things to work out, but it is no longer the essential aspect of your life. You have grown mentally, and you need to start focusing on yourselves. Think about how to achieve happiness. When things get out of hand in our relationships, we have a tendency to get upset and work hard to solve problems. We are so focused on making our partner happy that we neglect our own happiness. Do not tell yourself that you will be satisfied only when your relationship is repaired and you are back together. You must believe that you can be satisfied even without that relationship. Try to focus on activities that you can do right now that will bring you joy and serenity. Start as soon as possible to feel better. Finding the solution to the wrecked relationship should not be your sole and only reason for living. Do not consider it selfish to do something to keep your spirits up during this difficult time. If you saw your children or a loved one being happy, would you tell them to stop and focus on their problems, or would you be happy to see them beaming? Then why not treat yourself with the same affection and consideration? You deserve to be happy in your existence.

Allowing your partner to make mistakes is another step in recovering from the relationship. He or she may engage in foolish behavior, initiate inappropriate communication, become angry with you or file for divorce. We all make mistakes, including you. To be flawless and never make mistakes is not part of being human. You must make an effort to identify what hurts you. If you feel hurt, it is not necessarily because of another person's actions or words. It depends on how you interpret certain behaviors. You have different expectations about what this person should or should not have done. One person may say that he/she is hurt by his partner's infidelity and that he/she should not have done so. The one who cheated may respond by saying that he or she would not have wanted to receive only indifference and coldness, but a strong consideration of his or her feelings. In fact, the only thing people do all their lives is to try to be happy. So instead of feeling hurt, of saying my husband or wife should make amends, ask yourself a different and much more incisive question.... "Why did they cheat?" Also, "Is there anything I can do about our relationship?" Try to find a different interpretation for what happened. Finally, give it time. These events take time to improve, and things will definitely change. The current situation is not permanent. Soon you will have to make a decision, choose whether you want to continue and find reconciliation or whether you have had enough. It is not possible to say in general terms how long it will take for your relationship to return to normal, or whether it will ever reach the point where both of you will be happy together again. However, it is essential that you value each other and find a satisfying mental balance. This is the basis for facing any challenge and overcoming it. Focus on your own satisfaction first and foremost!

# 08
## WHAT TO DO TO GET HAPPY AGAIN

**W**hether the unfaithful person ever regretted his action is a question that haunts the mind of the betrayed. The partner may despair and regret it, or simply move on to someone else after experiencing so much pain. Generally, the betrayed person feels alone in his or her grief over the wrecked relationship. However, the unfaithful person also suffers. Even if he or she is the perpetrator of the betrayal, he or she feels sorrow for making someone with whom he or she shared part of his or her life suffer. There is no turning back, so one has to go in one direction, face the problem. To regain complete happiness, the betrayed person must give up the desire for revenge. The one who has betrayed will be responsible for his own suffering and will have to face his own responsibility. As Tim Keller wisely states, "If we really want to forgive, we must give up the desire to make him suffer as we are suffering." Therefore, forgiveness is essential to the journey to serenity. If someone decides to abandon you, it is his decision, regardless of his selfishness. However, if you stay together, you may both be disheartened and demoralized. You may keep thinking about how upset you are about the separation and blame yourself for falling in love with that person. Accept the pain and try to discover your new normal. Complaining to those around you is normal. Consider your emotions, and try to understand what is causing you the most pain. If you do not fully understand the source of the pain, you will not be able to overcome it and move on. Because of the loss, you may lose confidence in your ability to accomplish goals and be unable to discover love again. You are conflicted, and you keep thinking about whether you would still be happy together with that person. At this point you may even forget the cruelty, abandonment, and betrayal suffered during the relationship. Anger at the loss of one's dignity and values strikes a deep chord. However, you need to acknowledge and deal with it. To enter the next stage of your existence and find happiness again, you must face and overcome this pain. Therefore, forgiveness is essential for a healthy existence. The unfaithful person also experiences moments of extreme shame and humiliation. To avoid losing their dignity, they may appear more confident, aloof or indifferent. One of the most obvious distinctions between a happy relationship and one in crisis is how partners deal with mistakes. Everyone makes mistakes. Do we think that people in perfect marriages or relationships never make mistakes? Do they have no difficulties? Are they distinct and superior from the rest of the world? The reality is that even those in happy marriages make numerous mistakes. The key difference is how they are dealt with. There are some things you can do to reframe the mistakes in your relationship so that you can deal with them more effectively. The quality of your love depends on what you perceive to be error. It is irrelevant how big an error we perceive. It can be a significant mistake, such as cheating on a partner, or it can be small violations that negatively affect the relationship. It may be losing our temper, becoming furious, yelling at our spouse, being cold and uncommunicative, or refusing to consider his or her emotions. Refusing to address mistakes can have devastating consequences. It causes significant tension, and keeps the relationship in a state of negativity. If you focus on overcoming problems, you will receive more, but this includes effort and time. A relationally weak individual may experience emotional stress and feel inadequate. He begins to feel bad about himself, and may have cowardly behavior. This way of dealing with problems in a relationship, is the worst method.

Inadequate behavior can harm the relationship and create an imbalance of power. If you are the perpetrator and your partner is the victim, there is an imbalance between the two of you. This prevents the couple from being on equal footing. Mistakes have occurred in the past, and if you keep focusing on the facts, you will remain in the past. According to the dictionary, an error is a defect or lack that results from inadequate knowledge or negligence. Flawed is synonymous with imperfect. Remember that no one is flawless; mistakes are part of humankind! Being imperfect is the norm. It is obvious that if we are faced with a new event, we do not know how to react, because we do not know it. No one possesses complete knowledge. We can also make mistakes when we are negligent, heedless and careless. The repercussions of rash action, such as losing our temper or wanting to leave our partner, can be detrimental. At that moment our emotions can cloud our judgment. At this time we do not make decisions with logic, but with anger and rage. There are some elements that do not fit the definition of "mistake." First, if it was not done with malice toward the partner, it is not intentional because the repercussions cannot be predicted. It could have been a single incident or it could have been repeated several times, such as developing a negative attitude toward one's spouse. In any relationship, arguments are the norm; the difference between a happy or conflicted cohabitation is in ongoing dialogue and confrontation.

Acknowledge to yourself and your partner that something is not working. It is not necessary to justify your actions or give lengthy explanations as to why you acted as you did. It is sufficient to acknowledge to yourself and your partner that you are repentant. Then, it is not essential to apologize endlessly; once is enough. Stop reminding your interlocutor of the wrongdoing; it will have no positive effect. It prevents you from thinking correctly and having appropriate thoughts. Also, stop being responsible for your partner's emotions. If there is no constructive confrontation in a relationship, genuine relational harmony will never be achieved. We must accept complete responsibility for our feelings. Until you and your spouse learn to take responsibility for your emotions, you will not make significant progress toward a truly happy relationship. You are both adults and can learn to become more self-aware. If you do this your relationship will seem to truly transform. Try to see mistakes as a starting point and transformation to the positive. What has your mistake or your partner's mistake taught you? What are the positive things that can happen in the relationship after what happened? Mistakes are signs of what is not right in a couple. One must see the mistake as a warning. Continuing on the wrong path can have a disastrous effect on the relationship. Probably this not good period has made you realize that you have lost the joy and intimacy in your marriage. You have stopped doing those things together that made the relationship fun. Perhaps you have stopped appreciating your partner. This is like a wake-up call. A reversal requires a great deal of consciousness and a huge effort to remedy. If you still see a future together, you must not let the relationship slide. It is necessary to imagine a new meaning for the word mistake. To call it a fault is rather negative. It sounds like something wrong. Successful relationships perceive mistakes as a learning opportunity and a gift that has been given to improve life as a couple. If they are viewed in this way, they will be a huge opportunity to learn, grow and improve life. This will make your relationship better. People who have this mindset see things constructively and positively. Positivity takes over, and events are recognized as an opportunity for growth. Thomas Edison tried several times to build a light bulb. Many people asked him if he ever felt despondent after failing. He replied that he could not figure out what did not make it work. After several attempts he succeeded. Finding out what didn't make it work was an acceptance that he had made mistakes. Making the right corrections led him to one of the greatest inventions. Acceptance of flaws can be critical to the well-being of your relationship.

Consolidate the foundation of your relationship, regardless of the problems that plague it. What determines happiness, is not what happens, but the meaning we attach to the things that happen around us. By changing the meaning attached to your partner's past mistakes, you will begin to act differently. Is it possible to save a relationship when the partner has already filed for divorce or left? Being in the situation where your partner has packed up and filed for divorce is devastating. It is a reality that leads to the thought that the relationship may really be over. It feels like the end of the memories you shared and the future things you wanted to share. The time has come to make decisions about your life and your future. You are single again. Accept the moment, even if you feel terrible and life seems without a future. It is important to fight. The situation is now compromised, but never give up the idea of saving the relationship. Some couples reunite even after weeks, months or even years of separation. In some cases, there are even those who divorce and remarry with another person and then get back together. So, the bottom line is that it is never too late to save your relationship. Yet, the reason the relationship would end for good is that as time passes, you realize you are much happier without that person. You realize that you are able to find joy and well-being, with others or somewhere else. The most important aspect of your life is that you are happy.

It should also be considered that even if other people come into your life, the emotions that your partner has felt for you in the past can be felt again. If you want to take your partner in your direction, despite the fact that he or she has left you, may be possible if you both put in effort. You will have to be very strong to make it work without giving up and without finding your happiness elsewhere. You will have to make better decisions, and stop looking backward. Questioning your current position by looking at past mistakes will create negative feelings. Feelings of guilt, shame, anger, resentment or depression will envelop you. None of these feelings will help your condition, but rather make it worse. You begin to look to the future. Do you think obsessively about your partner? Thinking about it all the time does not help you achieve it. The key aspect is positivity and confidence. This will put you in a better mental position to win your partner back. Be positive when you are in their presence. You must be upbeat, cheerful and pleasant. Do not allow any negative feelings or energy to creep into your relationship. Remember that your behavior will make a great impression on them. Positivity is contagious and will make a big difference.

Another important aspect is to get out of your current situation. Do new things, such as choosing new hobbies. Surround yourself with people who make you feel good. It is very rewarding to take control of your life to create a positive future. Positivity leads to feeling better. After events like these, many people think divorce is the best thing that ever happened to them. They realize the true meaning of being happy. This does not mean that you have to have the same thought, but you have to judge your own situation. Focus on your happiness, and you will begin to feel better. When you live being honest and true to yourself, you become attractive to the world. When the estranged spouse sees you living a happy life, he begins to find you much more attractive than before. He may begin to wonder what he is missing. He may also begin to miss being a part of your life. Many people have experienced difficult separations and catastrophic events in their existence. However, many of them agree that the worst things that happened to them were in some ways the best things that could ever happen. Struggles make you grow and make you stronger. Instead of simply following a routine, start living through your authentic self. You may find it difficult to overcome your anxieties. The higher the quality of your character, the better your existence will be. The more you face adversity, the more resilient and strong you will become. In this way, you will attract positivity for yourself. Therefore, much depends on your mental attitude, your beliefs and the emotional strength you develop.

When relationship problems arise, you have to make choices. After a betrayal, you may be faced with four scenarios. The first is when you forgive your spouse and are ready for reconciliation. Under these assumptions you are very likely to end up getting back together. The second is when you may reconcile, but you are unable to forgive him or her. This is the point where you are stuck in negative thoughts and have to try to get through the bitterness and face reality. The third scenario is when you have forgiven but have not reconciled. This is the time when you are waiting for the last impulse, a sign from heaven or a lifesaver, to get through the transition and find the strength to get back with your partner. Inside, you have forgiven him, but you are waiting for him to repent more and then take him back. The last situation you may find yourself in is when you do not reconcile or forgive. This is unfortunately the end of the relationship. The time when you seek the intervention of lawyers to file for divorce materializes. Regardless of the situation you are in, learn to put your happiness above all else. It is the fundamental and most important thing. Start paying more attention and care to yourself, because it is the basis for having a fulfilling and peaceful life. With this foundation, it will be easy to share existence with a person who will enrich your future. Current partner or new love it may be.

# |09
## HOW TO SET UP RELATIONSHIP RECOVERY

**H**ere are some examples of situations people have encountered in their lives, and suggestions on how to rehabilitate or react after discovering the truth.

"He cheated on me and refused to take responsibility for his actions until I put him under pressure. I discovered other betrayals, and he adopted the same justifications. Now he is trying to reconcile with me and claims to be a different person." It is commonly thought that the victim is the only one agonizing and in need of healing. However, even the perpetrator of the betrayal may close in on himself, due to remorse over the betrayal, and place the "blame" on the victim. This behavior may be a consequence of narcissism or the individual's fear of commitment. The betrayed person, in turn, must try to understand his or her own emotions and feelings. The anger and pain, caused by events such as these, must be understood and dealt with carefully and rationally. Verify the repentance of the one who committed the betrayal, and do not rush into it. You can consider maintaining a constant conversation and discuss the other person's behavior.

"My ex-boyfriend cheated on me, lied to me and physically assaulted me. A month after giving birth to our son, I found out about his affair. Only after months, he admitted the affair after repeatedly denying it. We had a serious relationship for ten years, so it is all very painful. He put all the blame on me, and even had the audacity to deny the paternity of our son. I told him that he was the only person who had ever touched me, and I am willing to subject my son to DNA testing to prove to him that he is the father. He repeatedly accused me of deceiving him, when he was the one cheating." All of this is incredibly distressing. This is one of the most delicate situations because an infant child is involved. Having a child while dealing with these events makes everything much more complicated.

The first step is to get assistance or contact a trusted family member or person. Abandonment and indifference from a partner can be overwhelming. A pregnant woman is already going through a delicate period in her life. The priority should be to cut ties with the cheating partner and find a welcoming and loving environment for the newborn. Next you should consider whether to seek a dialogue with the father of your child. Now the priority should be the well-being of the child. The time for lawsuits and lawyers is not now; you will evaluate at a later date. In case, the other person will think of abandoning all responsibility; do not be alarmed, you will be enough. A large number of children are raised with the love of only one parent. To discharge inner emotions, it is advisable to visit a psychiatrist and undertake a long and effective therapy. Especially when an infant is involved, mental balance can be an important factor. Organize your life with the help of your loved ones and avoid anything that reminds you of your unfaithful partner.

"When my ex-wife's cheating became apparent, she abandoned me and our children. She drank and stayed out of the house, leading me to believe that the problem was solely alcohol. Following the divorce, I discovered that my ex-wife exhibited a hidden narcissism. She never gave me a specific explanation of why she divorced me, except that 'I had changed.'" This makes no logical sense. In a relationship, most women desire emotional support, fairness, friendship and sensitivity. When starting a relationship with a person, it is essential to know and understand them. A woman desires a man who is good-hearted and committed to the relationship. Other characteristics, such as economic status or beauty, may take a back seat. She desires someone who loves her unconditionally and can return her affection. However, if a relationship begins to fail, signs should be looked for. However compatible a couple is, the relationship will suffer if there is a lack of communication between the partners. Ignoring the other person in a relationship only serves to increase distance. It is difficult, but the key is to really understand what the other person expects from you and make a decision based on whether you can meet his or her expectations. Otherwise, it is a waste of time for both parties.

"My partner of five years told me that in recent months he has been cheating on me with another woman. He stated that he did it because he was dissatisfied with me. I have done everything possible to ensure this man's well-being. I have been close to him on many occasions, including the death of his father. Our disagreements centered on his constant night outings, drinking, as well as the fact that he did not spend enough time with me. He could not make me feel special. When I would ask him for explanations, he would describe me as 'annoying and boring,' which led him to be unhappy and look for another woman. I always felt that he was cheating on me, but he labeled me as crazy and always denied all my accusations. Even now I wonder how he could give love to another woman, who is not me."

It is unbearable to see the person you loved so much turn their back on you. Instead of cheating and blaming the other party he could have ended the relationship honestly. Betrayal can devastate anyone's soul and it is very common to feel humiliated and abandoned. The wave of emotions that washes over you can overwhelm you. It can be helpful to understand, to remember the moments in the relationship when the betrayer changed his or her feelings. Most likely, if the victim reflects, he or she will find that the other party never showed the same level of affection and love. After the initial trauma of betrayal, the betrayed person develops a fear of commitment because his former partner is too present in his life. The victim must recognize that she must move on and not allow self-doubt to cloud her thoughts. She must regain confidence and love for herself. This is the foundation for overcoming the trauma and finding new love in the future.

"Many years ago I was deeply in love with a man and believed we would get married. When he left me, I went into depression and even thought about suicide. It took me two years to recover from the trauma. Now I am happily married to another man, who is wonderful and caring. I rarely think about my ex, and I am sure I have forgiven him because I no longer hold a grudge against him. I hope he has found his way. It is a cliché, but time heals everything." This testimony highlights how reaching maturity leads to preventing emotions from taking over in a given situation. The adrenaline coursing through your body after a betrayal causes you to shut down or become aggressive. You may be so depressed that you think about suicide. However, holding on to something positive at such times is a very good idea. To achieve balance in your life, you must be motivated by a strong mind and a desire to live more independently. Take this situation as a growth experience and do not allow it to paralyze or permanently damage you. This will probably not be the only or the last relationship you have in your life. You must focus on regaining your self-confidence and understanding what you are worth. You must not allow anyone to exercise control over your life. You may have the feeling that you are left alone. This is an irrational fear created by the mind, which makes one perceive the other individual as irreplaceable. However, a person may come into your life who can love you even more than your former partner loved you. A soul with whom you can live the life you deserve. Being betrayed by someone who professed his great love for you is the worst thing ever. Despite this, many people decide to give the relationship another chance and forgive the betrayal. With the passage of time they show progress and a firm reconciliation. This is a possible event, but it requires several factors at once. Fundamental is forgiveness on the part of the betrayed. All this can result in a relationship with much more solid communication, understanding and affection.

A happy and fulfilling marriage is possible, but difficult. In a solid marriage, adverse events are just around the corner. There is no instruction manual on how to overcome the obstacles that will arise. Spouses must understand each other's needs and, most importantly, communicate effectively. Communicating can sometimes be difficult, but the better the communication the less conflict. The decision to reconcile with a person who has deceived you is a personal decision. It must be a thoughtful choice made with rationality and wit. Staying together amid misunderstandings and quarrels is not a good idea. It can have negative consequences for family, friends and children. If a couple stays together without the right assumptions and common goals, they make a huge mistake.

"It took me three years to forgive and five to trust my husband again. Now we are a happy family and live a peaceful life with our two children." Again, reconciliation can only be achieved if the cheater shows true repentance. When one partner cheats on the other, it is wrong to think that the relationship is always irretrievably over. In relationships, betrayal can be considered by far the most difficult obstacle to overcome. When a third person enters a relationship, he or she becomes part of the couple's life. It is difficult to overcome the feeling that your partner has allowed another person to enter your relationship. However, it is possible to recover the relationship, but it is essential to regain trust. The unfaithful partner must make a commitment not to make the mistakes of the past again. It is extremely difficult to recover a relationship, but not impossible. However, the goal can be achieved by creating an environment full of serenity, esteem, trust and hope.

# 10

## I STILL BELIEVE IN OUR RELATIONSHIP

You cannot bear the idea that the relationship is over. You continue to believe in the relationship in which you have placed your dreams. You long for your partner to forgive you and abandon his resentment. You want to give your marriage a second chance. You feel that you can overcome this challenge. Your spouse has no intention of forgiving you and cannot overcome the pain he or she is experiencing. Overcoming the pain and resentment is the first step to recovering the relationship. You have admitted your faults, so it is up to you to seek mediation to arrive at a favorable solution. Your partner has suffered public humiliation and experienced excruciating pain. Because of what you have done, they resent you and continue to regard you with contempt. People disappointed by the wrong behavior of those they loved tend to shut down their emotional world. They feel contempt toward their spouse because they feel betrayed deep down. There can be a communication gap, a lack of intimacy, and these are some of the main causes of the growth of negative emotions. The betrayed person does not want to be touched, hugged or kissed. Sometimes they state that they feel a real physical revulsion for their partner. They tend to prioritize other things over the relationship. They believe that other realities are more important. This could be their offspring, other family members, friends, or their own work. Ideally, the relationship should be one of the most important aspects of existence. Betrayal relegates the relationship almost to the bottom of the betrayed person's priorities. This situation can lead one to think that it is almost impossible to earn forgiveness. In most cases, a marital war begins. The partner who has been betrayed seeks every opportunity to bring suffering and upset into the spouse's life. They may alienate you from your children, family members and close friends. Many may start spending large sums of money. This is called financial sabotage. The intention is to hurt the other person after receiving. An almost insurmountable barrier is created. This toxic environment makes communication, trust and intimacy impossible. Therefore, it is necessary to remove these obstacles in order to seek possible forgiveness. Monitor your partner's behavior and begin to analyze the degree of resentment. This can provide guidance on how to proceed. The first circumstance that may arise is when your partner wishes to forgive you but does not know how to do so. He acknowledges his great pain, so he is unable to forget. In this situation you need to ask yourself some questions. Does the inability to reconcile affect his mood? Does he seriously want to do something about the relationship? Does he want to overcome the hurt and resentment he feels toward you? An initial analysis can give you a sense of what the margins are for reaching a positive conclusion. Another rather common form of resentment is when someone refuses to forgive you, even though they claim to want to do so. They are in a position to use their obvious suffering as a means of punishing the other party. They say, "I will not forgive you until you suffer punishment for hurting me." Therefore, they will punish you by continuing to make you suffer, knowing that this will cause great pain. It is an attempt to maintain control over you and the relationship. The intention is to externalize how you feel, but this can quickly become harmful. You must assess whether your partner really has a desire to absolve you. You will be able to answer this question relatively easily based on their behavior, emotions and actions. True forgiveness is the elimination of all suffering and signs of inner pain. To forgive, it is necessary to eliminate all traces of suffering associated with the source of the hurt. It must be unconditional. It is about metabolizing what happened and sticking together while holding back the impulse to leave the relationship. This is the ultimate goal. It is achievable.

Let us begin by saying that you must feel remorse for your wrong and repent for the actions you have done. The adultery must cease without compromise. You must cut all ties with the other person. You cannot realistically expect your partner to absolve you if you are not repentant. If a spouse deceives his wife six times and she forgives him each time, he will eventually stop forgiving her. There must be true repentance and a desire not to hurt your partner again. If you have an overwhelming instinct to cheat repeatedly, you must identify the underlying motivation. It is not a matter of forgiveness, but of dealing with the problem. Regarding forgiveness in cases of infidelity, you need to dispel several misconceptions. Believing that time will heal the relationship and restore it to its former glory is distinctly false. It is often used as an excuse not to engage in recovery. The individual indulges exclusively in self-pity. However, as with any other change, recovery from pain can happen quickly or take longer. Those who have been betrayed must sincerely and deeply forgive. To achieve this, an appropriate environment and mindset are needed. With this in mind, recovery can occur relatively quickly. In any case, it is necessary to allow the necessary time. Another misconception is that the betrayed person is responsible for recovery. Many people say..."It's their problem, I'll give her time to absorb the situation and metabolize." Nothing could be more wrong! The assumption of responsibility by the unfaithful individual is crucial.

The problem is that if the victim is left alone to deal with the situation, he or she may not know what to do and the timeframe may lengthen, or in the worst case go so far as to ask for termination of the relationship. Explain that you leave them time to deal with the situation, but that you will be there to assist and support them every step of the way. Wait for their return, but watch for progress as it happens. However, this should not be interpreted as constantly apologizing and oppressing them. Therefore, you must strike a balance to manage the situation effectively. Give them all your readiness. You are weakening yourselves, which in turn weakens the situation as a whole. What can you do to try to gain their forgiveness? Make sure that you do not take responsibility for their emotions, but leave it up to your partner to make the final choice. They may not want your help, but that does not mean they are not seeking a solution. Genuine forgiveness will have to come from deep within them. Reassure them that you will make sure this does not happen again, and that your only desire is to recover the relationship. You cannot force them to forgive you, even if you say you love them. They have to get over the trauma in their own time and by their own standards. You may have a huge burden on your shoulders and be consumed by remorse that will make you lose sleep. You have made a mistake. Everyone makes mistakes, but few admit their faults. This in no way negates the mistake, but you must acknowledge and correct the problem. Acknowledge to your partner that you have done an ignoble thing, and that you will do everything so that the relationship will improve and return to its previous state. Do this with strength and authority so that they know you mean business. The next step is to ask them to acknowledge that both you and they are human and fallible. Do this in a non-confrontational and general way. Tell them that you have made mistakes, but they make mistakes too. You are not accusing them, but you are seeking constructive confrontation. You are persuading them to recognize an alternative explanation for the event. In a couple there are always two perspectives for every situation. Hopefully, the effect of your actions will reduce some of their resentment and assuage some of their concerns. They may begin to realize that you are not solely responsible. You have committed a sin, but that does not have to erase all the positive things you have built together. The final step is to create an environment conducive to healing. When there are numerous problems in a relationship, it creates an atmosphere full of anguish and unhappiness. After making it clear that it is their responsibility to work on healing, the next stage is to move on. It is no longer necessary to focus on this issue. Forgiveness at this point should have been granted. Focus on creating a positive environment. Avoid dwelling on negative things. Whatever you aspire to accomplish, you will accomplish it. If your partner appears angry, it is appropriate not to apologize. You do not have to keep apologizing to them, only support them. Just shift the emphasis to this aspect. Another method is to be endearing. Show your mental strength. If you are optimistic and joyful, and not cynical, everything will be easier. Now you can be hopeful about the future. Do not dwell on difficulties. You need to show affection to your partner, but not in a weak way. You must restore the state of things before the betrayal.

About 44% of married men and 34% of married women have had an extramarital affair at some time in their lives, according to a study. Younger people are more likely. However, it can happen at any stage. How crucial is honesty in relationships? From childhood we have been taught that honesty is crucial. In a relationship it has an even deeper and more powerful meaning. A relationship involves two people living as if they are real and authentic, without fear of repercussions. It requires partners to reciprocate unconditionally. Are you living an authentic life? Are you yourselves? Consider the example of a person you contemplate. What sets you apart from the rest of us? I think one of the reasons we are attracted to these people is that they live their authentic lives despite criticism or negativity from others. They are happy to be themselves and are themselves. Fear is something that tends to hinder our relationships. Fear of what might happen, including fear of being criticized, hurt or making mistakes. We need to get to a point where there is no fear that genuine honesty will occur. When this happens, we need to allow the other person to be himself or herself. Allow him to make his own mistakes so that he can discover what is authentic to him without being harmed.

Can you imagine a relationship where you can say whatever you want without harming the other person? Can you imagine the immense positive impact it will have on you and everyone around you? You will be able to live your life developing yourself and never feel judged by others for doing so. If you fear that your partner is not being completely honest, the first point to watch is yourself. You must ask yourself clear questions. Why do you think he is not sincere? Are you able to express your emotions without fear of repercussions? Do you live your authentic life without fear? Perhaps you are not aware of the degree of honesty that can be achieved in a relationship. This can greatly improve your relationship. Ask yourself the following... Are you able to communicate every thought you have? Is there any idea that you have been unable to communicate to him/her? If your spouse asks you what you are doing or thinking, do you always tell him or her the truth? Have you ever thought about telling your spouse something, but refrained from doing so? Have you had multiple sexual fantasies, and failed to inform your partner? Are you able to provide a detailed explanation without feeling embarrassed? Honest marriages are few. So do not feel guilty if you are not a part of it. The first step is to determine the position and degree of honesty in your relationship. You will feel confined if you do not have a relationship based on complete honesty. You cannot be completely happy because you keep your emotions bottled up and do not express them. When you are dishonest with your spouse, there are huge consequences. There will be miscommunication between you, and the whole concept of collaborative development will be absent from the relationship. You must be allowed to make mistakes and grow from them. If you are unable to do this, you will reach a saturation point and the relationship will no longer be solid. It is worth committing to an open and honest relationship. You will be able to realize your own happiness. You will not need to "try" new things. You and your partner will be united and you will be able to have the most desirable experiences in life together.

# 11

## TEN STEPS TO HAPPINESS

The following chapter is a set of tips and "homework" to help you understand, process and overcome betrayal. It should not be seen as a foolproof method to solve all the problems in a relationship. Nothing will be able to wipe away the suffering suffered and the events that have occurred with a flick of the wrist. If a relationship has failed and has no more room for recovery, no book or therapist will be able to make it flourish again. These ten points will let you know if your relationship has a future or if it is time to think about yourself, and organize your life with other priorities.

**1)** Determine if forgiveness is warranted. This is a crucial step. Before you begin any journey, you need to figure out whether it is worth it. No matter how much you may adore a person, the most difficult challenge you face is to forgive a betrayal. The cheating partner will adopt a wide variety of excuses to justify his/her act. "It happened only once." ... "I drank too much, ended up in bed with another person..." "You neglected me and I found refuge outside the relationship."

In most cases, the partner regrets what happened, is disheartened, and would do anything to show repentance. If you believe you have a really special relationship, it is best to resist the temptation to separate and try to find a solution. Especially if you have been together with this person for a long time and your relationship is healthy and intimate, do what you can to recover it if that is your desire. Obviously, the discovery of betrayal will cast doubt on your entire past, but before making a decision you should analyze the whole situation. Make the necessary considerations. But never grant forgiveness to a serial cheater; he/she is not worth it. If he has done it before, it is likely to happen again. It may be the first time you catch him, but it is almost certain that he has cheated on you before. Also, if you are in a new relationship with someone, do not condone a betrayal. On this basis it will be almost impossible to form a solid relationship. Betrayal is a sign of a relationship that is doomed to fail, make no effort. A relationship that is not based on trust and respect has no future. It is likely, during a relationship, to be tempted to transgress. In these moments focus your attention on the bond you have, and what you risk losing if discovered. In order to have a complete forgiveness process, you must acknowledge repentance as sincere, and you must no longer think about the past. It is essential that it is not a simple compromise and that you are fully satisfied. There is no point in staying in the relationship and constantly making the other person feel guilty or expecting them to apologize at every opportunity.

2) After the initial pandemonium, take time to calm down and process. It is not appropriate to argue or fight immediately. This could make the situation worse for both you and your unfaithful partner. Walk, go to the gym or suffer in your room. Try to distract yourself as much as possible. At this stage, you may also be inclined to hurt yourself. Align yourself with these emotions and think logically. Do

not act impulsively and without reasoning. This period may last several weeks, so you should separate from your partner. If you live together, you should go stay with a friend or relative or in a hotel. Take a rest period and stop all communication. Try to understand why it happened, and how you could have missed it for so long. After taking some time to process the situation, you will be ready to deal with them. At this point, you may be full of doubts and worries, so it is better to create distractions for yourself than to think too much. You may feel the urge to communicate with the person, but it is preferable to refrain in order to regain serenity. Do not reproach yourself; it was not you who committed the impropriety.

**3)** Do not believe that your spouse has cheated on you because you are unattractive, because of your job or because children have become your primary concern. The person who cheats is responsible for the betrayal in almost its entirety. However, every person can make mistakes; we are human. But no reason is sufficient to involve someone other than your partner in your existence. The unfaithful partner can manipulate you by deflecting attention to your mistakes. He/she looks for excuses not to admit that he/she is the only culprit. If a couple encounters problems, they must try to solve them. If they cannot overcome them properly, they should separate. There is always the possibility of breaking off the relationship if both of you are not satisfied. When you are not satisfied with your partner, you must take responsibility for the decision to leave. Shortcomings and problems need to be discussed before reaching an irreparable situation, which in most cases ends in betrayal. Discussions should be constructive, but if they do not lead to any results, you can end the relationship and go your own way. Never allow the betrayer to hold you responsible. If this happens, cut ties without hesitation. Do not try to retaliate by cheating on your partner. Giving him/her a taste of the same medicine is a behavior that brings no benefit.

4) Money and financial problems can destroy a relationship. A change of circumstances may occur, such as loss of job, increased living expenses, money shortfall in the joint account. Another problem can

be the growth of our expectations and needs. There is nothing wrong with wanting more, but it is very easy to get into debt. Debts can start piling up, and before you know it the pressure becomes intolerable. Ironically, people increase their purchases when they are under stress, which traps them in a vicious cycle. If there is a lack of fulfillment in life people look for methods to relieve the pressure, they may book a trip or go to a movie or restaurant, which can make them spend more and make the situation worse. At the beginning of a relationship there are no financial obligations, but if you decide to share life, you share everything, even the burdens. You have common goals and things you wish to accomplish together. A significant part of our existence is devoted to financial fulfillment. You desire to buy a nice house where you can raise your children, and you seek a certain lifestyle. As these desires multiply, the financial impact increases. Expectations for spending will be greater because if you buy a house you will also have to buy items to fill the empty spaces. If you have one child, you may already be thinking about the second and third. Living nowadays is an expensive undertaking. In particular, men and women react differently to financial pressures. Women deal with this concern by seeking dialogue with their partners. They express their emotions through words. This is a completely opposite reaction to that of men, who usually shut down when under financial pressure. Men have the idea that it is their sole responsibility to solve problems in a relationship. They are biologically predisposed to achieve goals for a perfectly stable life. In caveman times, man's role was to hunt for sustenance. Therefore, having unresolved financial problems can be detrimental to their machismo because it affects their self-esteem. This is a generalization and may not be true in all cases. However, you can see some patterns of this behavior in your marriage. You need to realize if they are simply trying to deal with the problem on their own and do not want to involve you. If you find that financial pressures are affecting your marriage, be more aware of how you deal with the problem. You might consider your financial burden as something you can deal with individually and not let it affect your marriage. Think about not having to share everything with your spouse, keeping the marriage neat, and think that it is the right solution. Instead, you should acknowledge the problem, not push it aside and pretend it does not exist. Don't try to stifle the issue. Start having financial education. Start setting goals in the family sphere. You can sit down with your spouse and plan the goals you want to achieve together. Check your assets and pay off debts if you have any. Set a deadline for when you intend to pay off a debt or accumulate a certain amount of savings. The next step is to reduce expenses and increase savings. Determine what you can eliminate and what is unimportant. This process will reveal that you have begun to value money. After that, you can try to increase your income. Today you can do this in many ways. You could ask for a raise or find a second job. You can also sell items on eBay or conduct business online. There are many pleasant new ways to increase your income. The next step is to agree with your partner on a set of shared purposes for which you both take responsibility. It is essential that both parties refrain from assigning blame and actively meet each other's demands. If you are a woman and are not already actively involved in instilling financial values, you can do so. You can offer your husband suggestions and advice. To avoid this being the reason for the end of your relationship, men must agree to share responsibility.

5) Make sure that your partner is eager to recover the relationship. If you decide to forgive him/her, you will need to make sure that he/she is serious about wanting to get back on track with you, even if it takes months or years to start feeling good again. There is a significant distinction between saying and feeling sorry. Make sure that he or she is not faking it and that he/she is truly willing to stay with you. You can achieve real happiness if you stop being intimidated by the fear that your relationship will end at any moment. If the idea of separation makes you feel anxious, angry or depressed, you are likely to have some fears about it. This is not a judgment, because worries are completely normal. However, these worries do not help you achieve serenity. Security and emotional fears are common among people who want to divorce. Where would you go to live if you get divorced? This is one of the most common safety concerns. How will I make a living,

raise children and lead a comfortable lifestyle? How will the children react to a divorce? Men may fear that their finances will be affected and that their spouses will hire experienced lawyers. Emotional fears may relate to social consequences if divorced. Some of these fears are: "What will friends, colleagues, and family think?...Will I be able to maintain friendships?...Will my children still love me?...Will I be able to find a new love?...Is it painful to divorce?" These are the questions asked by a person who has the idea of divorce. However, if there is the will to save the marriage, you must stop worrying about its end. If you fall into the downward spiral, it will be very difficult to recover your relationship. This condition can push you to do all the wrong things rather than the right things. People tend to believe that everything will be fine along the way, just wait. But this situation does not last forever, because eventually a person gets tired of waiting if a change in his or her life does not come. It is necessary to be prepared to face any situation, whether negative or positive. Having overcome fear will help you cope better with the renewal process. Ask yourself if you have people close to you who love you, and if they can be of help at this time. Many times this aspect is crucial during a difficult time in a person's life. Create a positive image without the negativity of your spouse. Include only the positive aspects. This does not mean encouraging you to divorce or stay together, but it will make you optimistic and bring a breath of fresh air into your life. You will feel revitalized rather than vulnerable and discouraged.

**6)** You both need to acknowledge and accept pain. Communicate your emotions and make sure they are aware of your inner situation. Before you can restore the relationship, your partner must acknowledge that they have put you in a disastrous situation. Obviously they are not in a pleasant situation either, but make sure they understand you. Some couples have serious marital problems, they are unloved, there is no longer communication, and there is no longer sexual attraction. Of course, the biggest obstacle is when you have different plans about the relationship. The most difficult circumstance is when one partner sincerely wants to save the marriage, while the other does not. When one person is still clinging to the relationship and actively trying to rebuild it to make his partner happy, he believes that all problems will be solved. Although this may be true, many individuals prioritize their partner's satisfaction rather than their own well-being. Women especially put their own needs second. They prioritize their children and spouse, but become emotionally unhappy as a result. This is more harmful than beneficial. If you prioritize the needs of others over your own, you will end up distressed and stressed. You will go into depression, and your health, productivity and work performance will deteriorate. In addition, this can take a toll on relationships. Eventually you may resent your spouse. You have made a lot of efforts to recover, but you have not received anything in return or you are not getting the desired results. Being depressed and unhappy makes you look unattractive in the eyes of others. This will make both of you unhappy and the relationship cannot survive. Your soul is the most important element to save. In this context, spirit does not have a religious connotation. You must maintain and preserve the essence of who you are. What does it mean to be yourself? Start by engaging in activities that you truly enjoy. Devote your life and your time to activities that appeal to you. You must be free to express your opinions and say anything out loud without fear of being criticized. To please other people, it is essential to like yourself. With this foundation, your relationships with the community will be positive and constructive. And your relationships will also benefit.

7) Talk honestly about what happened. Do not address the problem hastily. It is not about disputing, but about discussing rationally. Ask what happened, and the reasons that led to the betrayal. It is not necessary for him or her to give intimate details, but he or she should reveal how often and when he/she saw the other person. Ask what he thinks about the other person. Your partner may tell you that he does not want to reveal anything, but you must try to get him to confess. Ask him if it happened long before you learned about it, so that you can gather more information before making a decision. Knowing the past is not always helpful, but by now the damage has been done. What's the worst that can happen?

Find out his opinion of the relationship and the scope for recovery. Find out why he deceived you and what his plans are for the future. Externalize your emotions and plans. At this point you have already communicated your wishes extensively, but after listening to the whole story, you may have changed your mind. Discuss how to make the relationship work. You might take notes and determine what mistakes to avoid, and what correctives to take to strengthen each other. Spend more time together, be honest or completely change your daily routine. You can consult a psychologist, discuss your problems with your friends, or work it out on your own. Establish guidelines. Should your partner change professions if he or she cheated on you at work? Many specialists agree. Should your partner contact you often when he or she is away from home? This may be demeaning, but keep in mind that you have already been humiliated and do not want to suffer the same thing in the future.

**8)** Do not obsess over the person with whom your partner has cheated on you. You may lose your mind and permanently destroy the relationship. If you know him or her and attend the same places or social events, you should avoid meeting him/her. Make an effort to ignore their existence. Do not compare yourself to this person or feel inferior to their supposed qualities. Do not condemn a person you do not know. They may have fallen in love with your partner, not knowing that they were already committed. Do not follow them on Facebook or other social networks in an attempt to understand what they have that you do not. Do not follow them in real life either. Also avoid talking about it with your partner. If you cannot control your obsession with this person, talk to an acquaintance, or consult a specialist. If you are carrying out all these controlling actions stop and prioritize the recovery of your relationship.

**9)** Work together to improve the quality of the relationship. Cheating is never justifiable, but it is likely to have occurred as a result of shortcomings in the relationship. Therefore, it is recommended to embark on a path of reconciliation that also passes through the sharing of daily life. Devote yourselves to a common passion or pastime. Share the same interests. If you have drifted apart because you have nothing in common, choose an activity that brings you closer together, such as a dance class. It may seem insignificant, but you will notice the difference. Make concessions. In a couple's relationship, both parties should benefit. All these new initiatives will be a breath of fresh air. A trip is not a permanent solution, but it will give you time to reflect and be alone. Stop blaming your partner. It may seem impossible and senseless, but if you want things to work out between you, you should not continue with the blaming. Do not obsessively insist that you feel endless and everlasting love for your partner. This is a counterproductive tactic. Be sincere and everything will work out for the best.

**10)** Commit to having more open communication every day. At least once a week talk about your authentic emotions. This action should not be forced, but neither should it be underestimated. Express your feelings to yourself and to your partner. Talk about both positive and negative emotions, even if the betrayal has shut you down emotionally. Do not get caught up in aggression. If you are furious, express yourself at the appropriate time. The recurring problem that people encounter when their marriage begins to fail is that they do not know what to do. Right now you are facing the possibility that your relationship will end. You have probably simply drifted apart. It has taken time, but you are no longer as connected as you once were. There is no longer satisfaction or pleasure in sharing life together. Have you started couples therapy to save your relationship? Have you discussed or attempted to discuss your problems with your spouse? Have you tried by "good" or "bad" means to achieve constructive dialogue? Have you tried to make them feel guilty? Determine whether any of these actions were successful. Did they have a positive effect? Did they bring you closer together or did they have the opposite effect? Did they put a strain on your relationship? If none of these methods work, it is very likely that there is not much room for reconciliation. Your partner, in addition to causing you pain, has little interest in recovering the relationship. At this point you need to prioritize yourself and care deeply about your present and your future. If things change, you will reevaluate the possibility of getting back together with your partner.

# CONCLUSION

When two people begin a relationship that often results in marriage they may be unaware of what lies ahead. Sometimes they may have trouble keeping everything in harmony or reconciling when problems arise. Love is something magnificent, but sometimes complex, and infidelity is even more so. To restore normalcy, it is essential to have something to hold on to. Some infidelities can be resolved quickly, while others can be difficult to resolve. People who want to rebuild their relationship after infidelity face a difficult journey. In the moment of destruction, one often no longer believes in love. One loses confidence in oneself and in interpersonal relationships. Infidelity of a partner is to be considered a bit like losing a part of oneself. Seek mental and emotional balance, and never give up hope. Accept the fact that the person abandoned you without giving you the answers you deserved. Even if you feel pain, move on. A prosperous and secure future awaits you. A healthy relationship free of resentment and infidelity consists of two people who are happy to be together and who support each other. Each of us should strive to reach the point where there is total respect and honesty in the relationship. If you believe that being honest is difficult or impossible, there are some behaviors you can adopt. Increasing the amount of honesty in your relationship will bring positive aspects. The first step is to be honest with yourself, and then be honest with others. Your relationship with others is a reflection of your relationship with yourself. If you want something in life, but believe it is not pleasing to your partner, discard this idea and ask yourself what you really want. Hiding something from your partner, even the most insignificant, can lead to confrontation if discovered. Never give up the idea of admitting a mistake and possibly apologizing. You may think he/she will be angry. Maybe he or she will or maybe they won't. But if he/she gets angry, deal with it and you will probably get over it. It is possible to live a peaceful and fulfilling relationship;

don't see it as a pipe dream. Set yourself the goal of sharing happiness with your partner. During a couples therapy session, a wife revealed that she wanted to go to a nudist beach, go scuba diving, and go boating. She was embarrassed to say it out loud because she feared her husband would judge her. Ultimately, it is critical to provide total honesty in relationships. The next step is to create an environment of complete trust and respect. Never make your spouse feel guilty for what they say or do. Do not judge their thoughts and feelings. Allow them to make mistakes.

Thank you for purchasing this book and I hope it was an interesting and educational experience. I put all my effort, enthusiasm and heart into every sentence I wrote. The main goal of this book is to help, with my experience, my readers understand and overcome betrayal, which is a deep and devastating malaise. I wish you the best success and hope that this reading has helped your soul to heal, and strengthened your relationship. Serenity and love.

Printed in Great Britain
by Amazon

40953444R00079